THE PHILIPPINES:
Shattered Showcase of Democracy in Asia

by Beth Day

Introduction by Carlos P. Romulo
Secretary of Foreign Affairs
Republic of the Philippines

M. Evans and Company, Inc. ⁄Æ NEW YORK, N.Y. 10017

The Philippines: Shattered Showcase of Democracy in Asia

M. Evans and Company titles are distributed in
the United States by the J. B. Lippincott Company,
East Washington Square, Philadelphia, Pa. 19105;
and in Canada by McClelland & Stewart Ltd.,
25 Hollinger Road, Toronto M4B 3G2, Ontario

Library of Congress Catalog Card Number: 74–78361
Manufactured in the United States of America
ISBN 0-87131-163-1
Design by Paula Wiener

9 8 7 6 5 4 3 2 1

Contents

Introduction

In the growing list of publications about the Philippines, Beth Day's book takes a preeminent place. It is a lucid and objective view of the Philippines today, in a time of transformations that stir Filipinos but often puzzle Americans.

To view the Philippines through Filipino eyes is, for an American writer, a task of insuperable difficulty. For this, there are at least three reasons. The first is the obstacle of a mental image of Filipinos created by a succession of well-meaning but frequently erroneous political and cultural "analysts." The second is the invisible but real cultural differences between Americans and Filipinos which fly-by-night reporters seldom perceive. And finally the need by American writers to tailor their observations to the understandable prejudices of their specific audience.

The consequence is a spate of books, articles and pamphlets that gall Filipinos as much as they misinform Americans. Outside of the specialists in certain fields of academic studies, American writers seldom compel, when they write about current events, the willing assent of Filipinos themselves who often feel that they have been "captured" by a camera that is badly out of focus. A question frequently asked by Filipinos when journalists write about the Philippines is, "What's his angle this time?," in a tone that suggests injured self-esteem and helpless skepticism.

From all these, Miss Day's book is a refreshing departure. As far as it is possible to do so, she has so to speak entered into the skin of Filipinos while retaining her American viewpoint. The recognition that a certain tension is bound to develop between points of view that are not irreconcilable yet are not similar results in a number of striking insights which will surprise even the subjects of this book.

Part of the author's success derives from the fact that she has refused to be misled by the superficial similarities in the culture of Americans and Filipinos. It is customary in the literature of the day to speak of the Coca-Cola culture, the Rotarian mentality, the Hilton complex, and not least, certain addictions (to drugs and to that other drug, television, among others) which are popularly supposed by foreigners to afflict Filipinos of all variety. In a certain sense, this is true, but only superficially. Like all assimilative races—and which are not?— Filipinos adopt the vices of other cultures for display while retaining an interior life which has proved to be singularly resistant to current modes, manners and fashions.

In any event, such vices are less pervasive than is commonly believed. Urban Filipinos, with their rather extensive exposure to influences from abroad, partly imbibed from an American-style education and partly acquired from the example of the movies, are prone to develop an affinity with them, just as they were in a previous era when the Spaniards were in the Philippines.

But the vast majority of Filipinos live as it were beyond the pale, and it is they who exhibit most visibly the traditional codes and systems of belief which govern their social and political conduct.

Americans who meet individual Filipinos to whom in ordinary social intercourse they grant small favors are often amazed if not thrown off balance by a show of gratitude so excessive that it is frequently mistaken for fawning. The fact is that gratitude, or *utang na loob*, is an important key to Filipino behavior.

Extrapolated on a national scale, this is an explanation for the notorious relationship between politicians and voters in a system of never-ending reciprocation of favors. The length of a politician's life is measured in terms of the favors, such as jobs or loans of money, he is in a position to give his supporters. In turn, the latter are obligated according to the code of *utang na loob* to keep the politician in office.

Even the relationship between landlords and tenants is frequently governed by the concept of *utang na loob*. The landlord who has once saved the child of a tenant from illness feels free to exploit the services of the tenant with perfect impunity, since he is protected by a code freely accepted by all within his society. Indeed, he would not even realize that he is exploitative, in much the same way that the practitioners of exploitative capitalism feel they only obey the laws of the system rather than merely indulge in personal caprice.

Observers who lack this background often ascribe such practices to an institution, namely, feudalism, but in this they would be only partly correct. As the institution withers away under the impact of modernization, the code remains, transferred to other areas of social life.

Investigations into the concepts underlying Filipino behavior such as the foregoing (only recently expounded by a number of brilliant Filipino scholars) emphasize the differences in the value systems between Filipinos and other peoples—in this specific instance, Americans.

In other words what others view as an aberration will be perfectly rational to the Filipino. Nowhere is this form of misunderstanding more widespread than in the case of the New Society recently established by President Marcos. Few deny the effectiveness of the reforms undertaken by the New Society, since the facts speak eloquently in this respect. But few understand the internal necessities which made the New Society imperative and inevitable.

In their fascination with western-style political institutions, they fail to see that these have been rendered obsolete in the Philippine context. In the exact forms in which they existed, they impeded rather than promoted national development. The New Society is essentially a strategy for modernization, and such being the case, sound tactics require the renovation of institutions in order to serve the aims of the New Society more adequately.

Miss Day's narrative takes full account of the factors, obscured in many other publications, that led to the establishment of the New Society. As sheer narration, the book is engrossing. The terrible events that preceded the twenty-first of September, 1972, are delineated with perfect fidelity to facts, facts that she accumulated through months of patient research and investigation in the provinces, in Manila and the libraries in Washington and New York.

As an author and as an interpreter of my country to the American people, I am impressed less by Miss Day's command of facts, excellent as it is, than by her sure and even-handed treatment of background which is often regarded as peripheral by other writers but is seen by Miss Day as integral to the discussion of contemporary events in the Philippines. I hope that this book will inaugurate an era of renewed understanding between Filipinos and Americans.

CARLOS P. ROMULO

THE PHILIPPINES:
Shattered Showcase of Democracy in Asia

1
The Summer of '72

On September 21, 1972, the Philippines's duly elected president, Ferdinand Marcos, stunned the liberal western world which had cherished the image of the former American colony as the "outpost of democracy in Asia" by declaring martial law—thus joining his small island domain to the growing list of independent Asian nations that have opted for an authoritarian government.

The President was forced into taking this drastic measure, he said, in order "to save the republic" which he claimed was under siege from both leftist and rightist factions and on the brink of a violent overthrow.

Communism has always been more than a mere threat in the Philippines, due in part to the volatile combination of a basic social inequality plus a spiraling population rate with its inevitable residue of restive unemployed youth. At the time that martial law was declared, the government military forces were engaged in active combat with the Communist New Peoples Army in northern Luzon, while at the same time they battled sporadically with the chronic uprisings among the dissident Muslim Filipinos in Mindanao to the south.

In Manila itself—heartland of the Philippines which contains nearly one-third of the country's urban population—an unholy alliance of the legitimately aggrieved youth and political activists, backed by the mischievous support of a status-quo press and the oligarchic elite who opposed all goverment efforts at reform at any cost (including the clear and present danger of a bloody revolution), had in the past two years turned the beautiful city into a frightening hotbed of demonstrations and random violence, earning it the doubtful distinction of being one of the most dangerous and lawless cities in the world.

Demonstrations that involved rockings and bombings had become an almost daily occurrence. Thousands of dissidents massed at every provocation—a not unlikely feat in a country where seventy percent of the population is under twenty-seven years of age. Some were spurred by political ideology, some by a rigid nationalism that opposed any foreign aid or investment, some merely joined the march for the day's wages or the free lunch provided by the affluent opposition to the administration. Targets of mass attack were not only government buildings, but also foreign embassies. Both the Vietnamese and the United States embassies were fire-bombed; the Israeli embassy was mobbed and several other embassies were placed under twenty-four-hour security and their ambassadors provided bodyguards at their own request.

In January 1970 when, after an especially bitter election, Marcos won an unprecedented second term, his reelection was greeted with an escalating wave of politically inspired anarchy and violence. On the day that he delivered his acceptance speech before Congress, as he and his wife came out of the building, their car was stoned and the President and Mrs. Marcos barely escaped injury. In the excessive reaction by the police that followed this attack against the President, five people were killed and three security men injured. Four days later demonstrators surrounded the presidential palace, Malacanang, and when the President gave orders to have them "hosed" away with water from fire trucks (rather than by the use of firearms) the mob succeeded in commandeering one of the trucks and smashing one of the palace gates before they were turned away. Within the ensuing twelve months there were seven known assassination attempts on the President's life.

One of the most appalling of the politically inspired outrages, in terms of needless death and injury, occurred in August 1971. A political rally staged by the Liberal party at Manila's Plaza Miranda was turned into a holocaust when bombs and grenades exploded on the outdoor speakers' platform—killing nine people and injuring ninety-six, among them the eight senatorial candidates who were present.

The aura of anarchy that enveloped the country was reminiscent of the dangerous days in 1950 and 1951 when the Huk* armies reached the outskirts of Manila and came within an ace of seizing the city. The ace in that case had been the then-Secretary of Defense Ramon Magsaysay, who succeeded in swooping down secretly on the Manila-based brain center of the operation—the

---

* Hukbalahap. *Hukbong Bayan Laban sa Hapon,* the People's Army Against the Japanese. Organized as a peasant guerrilla resistance army during the occupation, the Hukbalahap was the military arm of the combined agrarian socialist and communist parties in Central Luzon.

Communist politburo and secretariat—and arrested all the leaders, after which, temporarily rudderless, the Huk army withdrew in confusion, and the insurgency fell apart (a coup which did much to win the presidency for Magsaysay).

But the Communists had retrenched and replaced their leaders, and the New Peoples Army, which had failed in Central Luzon, was now alive and well in its new stronghold in Isabela province in northern Luzon—so strong, in fact, that it maintained its own "invisible government" which levied and collected taxes more effectively than the national IRS, which was hamstrung with patronage and corruption.

In October 1951 when President Quirino had learned of the existence of a Communist politburo in the city of Manila he had suspended the writ of habeas corpus in order to facilitate the Communist leaders' capture. Now, following the Plaza Miranda massacre, President Marcos did the same thing.

The Plaza Miranda culprits were never apprehended, however (and arguments rage to this day about who was actually responsible), and after a few months of uneasy quiet the suspension was lifted on January 11, 1972.

This restored freedom of action was greeted with a renewed rash of violence. In the succeeding five months, throughout the spring and early summer of 1972, bombs exploded in leading office buildings throughout Manila: at the Arca building on Taft Avenue, in the offices of the Filipinas Orient Airways, at the huge Philam Life Insurance building across from the Hilton Hotel on United Nations Avenue. . . .

Whether all this random bombing could be laid at the door of the Communist movement has never been clear. But on June 18 government forces captured a munitions ship that had run aground in Isabela province which proved to be loaded with foreign-made arms and ammunition destined for the Philippine Communist forces. Along with the arms, the government foray also turned up an interesting document: a New Peoples Army manifesto which detailed an assault on the Philippine government and outlined proposed violence in Manila apparently designed to paralyze the city and prove the impotence of the government to protect its citizenry.

If indeed the bombings could be laid to the NPA, a glance at their Isabela Plan shows that they were operating a little ahead of schedule. July and August called for the sabotage of schools and universities and robberies of banks that were "controlled by American imperialists." "Bombings of government buildings, embassies and utilities" doesn't appear on the agenda until September and October.

August 30 was an especially busy day for the bomb squads: they hit again at the Philam Life building, which had just cleaned up from the July third attack, and caused some damage to it—but even more to its neighbor, the Far East Bank and Trust Company. An armored car was blown up at the Philippine Banking Corporation. Bombs were detonated in the Investment Development offices and the Daily Star Publication building. Still another bomb—hastily placed—was accidentally defused when a door was opened in an office directly below that of Secretary of Foreign Affairs Carlos P. Romulo in the old Department of Foreign Affairs building on Padre Faura Street. If indeed President Marcos himself was planting bombs in order to justify a proclamation of martial law, as some of his political opponents later claimed, it seems rather unlikely that he would wish to assassinate his own Foreign Minister, or his Secretary of Defense, Juan Ponce Enrile, whose car was ambushed a few weeks later. (Since it was late in the day, Enrile had taken the precaution of riding in the second security car, and thus missed the twenty-one shots that raked the backseat of his car where he normally sits.)

The random bombing contained no clear pattern. Its prime motive seems to have been to paralyze the city and destroy faith in the government. The very sense-lessness of the choice of sites was enough to arouse hysteria: airline offices were bombed, banks, department stores. Grenades were tossed into the midst of one provincial fiesta. Bombs were exploded in the Sugar Institute, the Department of Social Welfare, the Manila City Hall. City water mains were blasted. The handsome new International Airport building was burned. The rooms where the constitutional convention was working on the new constitution in the Manila Hotel were bombed in June of 1972. And when the convention moved to cheaper quarters in the City Hall in neighboring Quezon City (the actual capital of the Philippines) the rest rooms they were using were promptly blown up and destroyed.

If the object of the bombings was to bring the functions of the city to a virtual standstill, they could be termed a success. Private citizens became afraid to go to stores to shop, to attend the cinema, or dine in public restaurants. The Spanish-born wife of an investment broker who lives in one of the midcity apartment buildings which escaped the 1945 bombing that leveled most of old Manila recalled, "I didn't dare walk two blocks to shop in midday. I had to call the car to be taken to a store across the street! There were so many of those huge showcase windows broken which had to be boarded up in the big offices in Ayala Avenue that we called it 'Plywood Avenue.'"

In reaction to such rampant lawlessness the carrying of firearms by private citizens became *de rigueur*. Among the irrepressible Manilans the standing joke was that you could tell a Filipino couple anywhere in the world: the woman bulged in front and the man bulged behind! Leading politicos began to behave like Chinese warlords, sporting, in addition to their own side arms, armed body-guards and even private armies (of as many as a thousand men) bristling with weaponry. Signs were posted at the entrances to restaurants and nightclubs—and even in the reception rooms of government offices: DEPOSIT YOUR FIREARMS HERE.

With government buildings the focus of so many of the attacks, government employees became skittish about going to work, and were apt to leave their offices at the first rumor of a bomb threat. Secretary of Education Juan Manuel admits that he attempted to keep some of the actual bomb threats a secret from his staff in order to "get the day's work done." "You would go to work at eight in the morning," he recalled those perilous days, "and around two or three in the afternoon you'd get a phone call: 'Be careful. There will be an explosion on your premises.' I'd go on working as if nothing had happened. But usually someone in the department found out about the call. And I'd look up to see all my staff running home. You couldn't keep a department function-ing in those days."

The Friday before martial law was declared the Superintendent of Public Schools in Manila went on the air at seven A.M. to announce that all classes had been suspended for the day because explosives had been discovered in some of the classrooms.

With the general breakdown of services and the overall demoralization of the city, crimes of every nature thrived. Kidnappings, car-nappings, robbery, street shoot-outs between crime lords, became a daily occurrence. As tales of such rampant disorder and lawlessness spread abroad, tourism—once an important source of income for the colorful islands—slowed to a trickle. Foreign investors —whose capital was desperately needed to launch the government's efforts at industrialization of the under-developed country—backed off, leery of the reputed corruption among the officials with whom they must deal, and the apparent instability of a government which could not control crime nor protect its citizens. In a memorandum to the President the day before he proclaimed martial law, Marcos's able, outspoken Annapolis-educated Executive Secretary, Alejandro "Alex" Melchor, warned that the deteriorating peace and order conditions were crippling the nation's economy. [In 1972 the GNP fell 3 percent.] If some drastic steps were not taken, Melchor predicted, the economy would suffer an irreparable collapse.

What tourists or investors the bombings, demonstrations, and street crime did not scare off, the newspapers did—filing daily florid accounts of all the unrest, spiced with virulent attacks upon the President and the First Lady, Mrs. Imelda Marcos (a political power to be reckoned with in her own right and an acknowledged "vote-getter," Mrs. Marcos was apparently considered fair game by the opposition). Politics sank to such a personal level that when Mrs. Marcos suffered a miscarriage and had to be rushed from the Palace to the hospital, the President bitterly blamed her condition on the unrelenting political harassment and invective which she had suffered, while his opponents spread the rumor that Mrs. Marcos was not pregnant at all and that her so-called emergency hospitalization was nothing more than another of her husband's astute political tricks—designed to win sympathy for his side.

Then, as though the gods had had enough of all this man-made disturbance below, the scene of political anarchy was crowned with a series of natural disasters that befell the Philippines late in the summer of 1972: first landslides killed twenty-five people in the lovely mountain resort and site of summer government at Baguio City. Then, in swift succession, earthquakes, fires, typhoons, and apparently endless flooding struck the rice-growing areas of southern Luzon, effectively inundating Manila itself as well as destroying a large section of the annual rice harvest. Ironically, while southern Luzon was being victimized by record floods, other agricultural areas in the verdant Visayas in the center of the Philippine archipelago were undergoing one of their worst droughts. Between the two extremes, so much rice was destroyed that there was no hope that the country could be self-sufficient in its major food supply for the following year.

The punishing floods in Luzon were likened by foreign correspondents to those described in the Bible. As the rains continued—without respite for forty days—families seriously considered building arks. In the city limits of Manila water ran waist-deep in many of the main thoroughfares and in some sections of the city transportation was reduced to wooden barrels, cut in half and paddled by hand. By the time the rains slackened, over one hundred inches had fallen, and crops, roads, bridges, and many work animals had been destroyed. There was a rice shortage, a sugar crisis, and skyrocketing food prices. Two-thirds of the country was a disaster area. Citizens who had stoically withstood the bombings panicked at the food shortage and stormed the stores, fighting over the remaining rice.

At 7:15 on the evening of Saturday, September 23, President Marcos went on national radio and television to announce his decision:

". . . I have proclaimed martial law in accordance with powers vested in the President by the Constitution of the Philippines.

"The proclamation of martial law is not a military takeover. I . . . use this power . . . to protect the Republic . . . and our democracy. A republican and democratic form of government is not a helpless government. When it is imperiled by the danger of a violent overthrow, insurrection, and rebellion, it has inherent and built-in powers. . . . Such a danger confronts the Republic. . . . Persons who have nothing whatsoever to do with such conspiracy and operations to overthrow the Republic of the Philippines by violence have nothing to fear. . . .

". . . I issued general orders for the government . . . to control media . . . as well as public utilities. All schools will be closed for one week beginning this coming Monday. The carrying of firearms outside residences without permission of the armed forces . . . is punishable with death; curfew is established from twelve o'clock midnight to four o'clock in the morning; the departure of Filipinos abroad is temporarily suspended. . . .

"It is my intention beginning tomorrow to issue all

the orders which would attain reforms in our society. . . ."

The proclamation had actually been signed by the President forty-eight hours before his official announcement—enough time for the military to begin rounding up thousands of the known insurgents.

September twenty-fourth Manilans awoke to a silent city. There were no armored tanks or sandbag barricades. Only a few soldiers were in evidence at key intersections. But the demonstrators were gone. The handguns had disappeared. The streets were safe to walk upon.

There was no news. The press was temporarily silenced. Congress was closed. The upcoming elections suspended. All citizens were subject to the new curfew—which cleared the streets from midnight until four A.M.

What had happened, the outside world wondered, to the friendly Philippines and its burgeoning hopeful dream of democracy?

What had gone wrong?

2

What Went Wrong

When a foreign observer looks at the Philippines the immediate question that comes to mind is, What happened? Why hasn't the Philippines prospered in these post-World War II years like its affluent southeast Asian neighbor, Thailand? Or Singapore, or Taiwan? Or its wartime enemy Japan?

The 7,107 islands that make up the Philippine archipelago are far from poor in either agricultural or mineral resources. The land is lush, fertile ("put a pencil in the ground and it will grow"). Food is abundant. Numberless varieties of vegetables and fruits are available year-round. Fish and shellfish abound in the inland and coastal waters. If the annual typhoons don't devastate half of the rice lands, as they did in that unfortunate summer of '72, the country produces sufficient rice to feed its ever-expanding population. Its rate of agricultural productivity is among the highest in the world. It is the largest individual supplier of America's sugar, the world's leading producer of coconut and abaca (hemp), a major source of supply for wood and wood products. Oil has been found in the Philippines and only awaits sufficient investment and technology to bring it in. There is enough volcanic power available to establish geothermal power centers which can supply limitless energy for both private consumption and industry.

Yet the Philippines has persistently lagged behind its Asian neighbors. A scene of constant political impasse and turmoil since it achieved independence in 1946, fortunes have been made there—by both foreign and domestic interests—yet the economy and social order has remained basically unstable and the mass of Filipinos have remained at poverty level.

Why is it that a country so blessed in natural resources has not developed them in a systematic fashion? Nor moved—as similarly endowed countries—from a basically agrarian to an agro-industrial economy, with its vast pool of available manpower? Why should such a productive and relatively unexploited land suffer from chronic unemployment and civil unrest?

More important to the American mind: why has the fledgling Philippine government, trained by Americans and patterned on sound American-style democracy, proved so precarious and ineffectual? Why has its efforts at badly needed social reforms always come a cropper?

And why, finally, has it been necessary for the country's survival, according to President Marcos, to give up the democratic dream and shift suddenly from a fumbling but functioning democracy to one more of the growing list of authoritarian governments? Why did Marcos feel that he alone could lead his country out of its wilderness of economic and social stagnation? Marcos had already had one full term in office under the old system, and very little to show for it. What did he think he could accomplish under martial law that he had been unable to do before? Why did he think he could do what no other Philippine president before him had been able to do?

In actual fact, the Philippines (contrary to some of the coverage by the foreign press which was apt to be fascinated only with the country's appearance of rudderless violence) has had some very good presidents—all of whom shared an understanding of the chronic colonial ills that plagued the little underdeveloped country. The Philippines's first president, Manuel L. Quezon, a fiery and charismatic nationalist leader, saw very well the need for restructuring what was basically a feudal society of rich and poor. His 1939 program of social justice (cut short by the outbreak of World War II) held much the same premise as the present administration's program for agrarian reform. Yet Quezon was to die in the United States before his beloved Philippines was freed, without seeing his program put into action. Following the wartime occupation by the Japanese, the Philippines had other presidents with similar vision: Osmeña, Quirino, Magsaysay had their plans for reshaping society which, in a single term in office and blocked consistently by political opposition in Congress, each was unable to carry out. Marcos's predecessor, Macapagal, was the author of a carefully thought out land reform program which he also was unable to implement but which serves as the basis of agrarian reform today.

One of the sad ironies of Philippine political life has been that the mass of citizens have always cherished the goals of freedom and democracy and they have been successful at creating strong democratic leaders and voting them into high elective office. Yet, in each instance, the form of government itself has defeated the reform efforts of the individual presidents. The three branches of government, instead of complementing one another, have, in the Philippines, achieved little but stalemate. While ideally a democratic Congress should share in the decision-making powers of a president, what a Congress actually does (as political writer Elizabeth Drew so aptly pointed out in *The New York Times,* September 23, 1973) is to "legitimize" a president's decisions. In the Philippines, however, the Congress has failed to perform either function—to share or to legitimize. Instead, it has consistently used its legislative powers to block its presidents' executive decisions. Even in so clear-cut a matter as the appropriation of funds for the flood victims of the 1972 disaster, the Philippine Congress balked and refused to pass legislation—with the result that the President was forced to look for foreign aid to fund the emergency rehabilitation of the flood-devastated areas.

Not only has the legislative arm routinely blocked the executive, but the judiciary also has often exercised a "passion for pure law" at the expense of desperately needed government progress. When the present land reform program was first implemented, during President Marcos' first term, wealthy landowners who did not wish to break up their holdings took the government to court and the matter stayed there—tied up in legal process with the peasants as landless as ever. Another classic case of judicial interference at the expense of national development was the now-famous Manila waterworks case. The government had managed to get a World Bank loan to improve the municipal water supply. Yet an individual pipe manufacturer in Manila was able to get a court injunction against the government agency in charge of the project so that for two years the government was unable to bid internationally for the pipes that were needed to commence it. The result was that not only was the community shortchanged on its water supply, but the government's good relations with the World Bank were jeopardized.

Since it achieved independence and proudly took title to the first democracy in Asia, a quarter of a century ago, the Philippine government has become infamous for graft and corruption, malversation of public funds, and self-partisanship in political parties. Each president who tried to put through reform programs for which he had hopefully been elected by the people found all his good words and promised deeds stymied by a recalcitrant, status quo Congress.

For indeed, the Congress of the Philippines has never been representative of the people. The majority of the political leaders (with the exception of the Presidents themselves) have all come basically from the same landed class, the power elite that was originally spawned under Spanish colonial rule, and once in power, they have used their political office to further their own wealth and privilege rather than serve the interest of their constituents.

As the country's national hero, the poet-patriot-martyr Dr. Jose Rizal, commented in the nineteenth century, in the Philippines there has been individual but not national progress. The Spanish legacy of feudalism showed not only in a basic inequality of land and wealth and power distribution, but also in a cavalier colonial social attitude. Despite its espousal of so-called democracy, the Philippines has never been a classless society. Four centuries of Spanish rule left a nation of Spanish masters and

Filipino serfs which, when the Spanish left, was soon replaced by an internal colonialism with the same pecking order. Filipinos fortunate enough (through crown grants or the acquisition of church lands) to take over from the Spanish masters soon became masters themselves, and a Philippine "400" developed which, like the Spanish overlords before them, had a monopoly on the country's resources, and were inspired with no nationalist passion to help develop their country. "To each his own" became the self-serving cynical motto of the privileged class.

"If you don't give the poor what is rightfully theirs, the time may not be far when you will not only lose all that is yours but you may even lose your very lives!" President Quezon warned the entrenched Philippine oligarchy thirty years ago. Yet the oligarchy, with a few outstanding exceptions, has persistently failed to heed that warning. Nearly all proposed programs for either tax or land reform have been blocked at the legislative level.

The Philippine Congress, in a unique perversion of the democratic ideal, has been consistently representative of the few rather than the many. Short of inherited wealth, the one clear-cut avenue to power in the Philippines has been politics. After the country achieved its independence following World War II it became fashionable for ambitious boys to study law as a stepping-stone to political power. And once in political office, the professional politicians settled down to stay, voting themselves large salaries and, in a system of political dynasty that became internationally scandalous, dispensing jobs, favors, government funds to families, relatives, friends, and protégés. Funds designated for government projects seldom saw their way past individual pockets. (Even among the

Filipino Muslims in the south it has now emerged that what little the government did allocate to the Philippines's largest non-Christian minority seldom reached the people, but was instead channeled into the personal interests of the Muslim politicians. To offset that, the government is currently dealing through Muslim teachers and religious leaders rather than politicians.)

Since all the politicians, the country over, were drawn from the same class, and as interchangeable as peas in a pod, the two-party system itself was rendered meaningless in the Philippines (the two major parties, the *Nacionalistas* and the *Liberals,* so the going joke went, were as separate and distinct from one another as Coca-Cola and Pepsi-Cola) and the politicians blithely shifted parties as easily as their shirts, depending on where at the moment lay the best guarantee of perpetuation of self-interest. There was little in the way of party allegiance and while the major motivation of most politicians in the world is, once elected, to stay in office, the Philippine politicians extended this principle to mean a lifetime of power and influence. "They took all the evils of the American system—and improved on them!" commented a diplomat acquainted with both the American and the Philippine Congresses.

This devotion to self-interest rather than to one's constituency or political party apparently showed up very early, judging by the sober suggestion of the republic's first president, Manuel Quezon, that perhaps the Philippine government might best serve its people if it were a partyless democracy.

Philippine elections became notorious for their corruption ("even the birds and the bees voted"), their violence, and their extravagance. Balloting in the areas controlled by the most powerful political warlords was little more than a polite bow to the democratic process carried out in routine feudal manner. Returns were often brought in the day before the election, by the barrio captains or teachers, who had been given their instructions by the lieutenants of the politician. "They told them, all right, here are the returns. You give our opponents so much and then this will be the result," explained Marco's Harvard-trained Secretary of Defense Juan Ponce Enrile, who is himself the product of barrio life. "There was no free balloting. Just as there was no justice."

Justice flew out the window as politicians' private armies watched over the barrio ballot box and the rule of the gun was so prevalent that rural elections were likened by observers to Hollywood westerns—or perhaps more accurately the gangsterism of Chicago's prohibition days. It was not unusual for several hundred people to be injured or even lose their lives in the course of a single election. "In the barrios, people could be killed like chickens," said Enrile, "and the family had no legal recourse. You don't know what it means to barrio people to find out there is a law beyond the landowner or the local politician."

In a country suffering from chronic poverty and un-employment, it was estimated that several presidential campaigns outspent comparable American campaigns by as much as four to one. Candidates who were not them-selves members of the wealthy elite "belonged" to either oligarchic or big business interests who could put them in power. The payoffs came later in the form of favorable legislation and patronage.

To be "anyone" or get "anything done"—even those services rightfully due the ordinary citizen—required political influence. Politicians were either members of the oligarchy—the top ten percent that controls ninety percent of all land and wealth in the country—or their handmaidens. No one could get a job, obtain a passport, build a house, or take a case to court on the basis of simple merit, need, or achievement. Even the military was dependent for its appointments (beyond the rank of lieutenant colonel) on political patronage. Everything had a price, from service promotions through department budgets. If an officer didn't have a patron, the accepted alternative was a cash payment. When Secretary of Defense Enrile appeared before Congress to request reinstatement of a budget cut for his department, he was told he could get it—in return for ten percent of the reinstated funds to the congressman in charge.

Patronage had become so entrenched as a way of economic and political life in the Philippines by the 1960s that it was practically impossible for a businessman to hire or fire on the basis of merit. "I'd been doing business in the Philippines for twenty-seven years," said Hans Kasten, an American importer and textile manufacturer. "But by 1970 I'd just about had it. I was thinking of closing down and retiring to Honolulu. You couldn't fire anyone with political protection, no matter how incompetent he was. And you had to hire people you didn't need. You couldn't turn around without facing another letter of introduction—to someone you didn't want. But if you refused the request, they'd block you if you needed government clearance for something. It got so that when I saw another fellow standing in my office with a letter in his hand I wanted to slam the door and run."

"A private business," explained Manila banker Peter Go,

"was forced to hire at least a hundred people that it didn't need and didn't want."

Patronage reached down to such lowly levels as janitors. At the time Carlos Romulo retired as Ambassador to the United States and came home to the Philippines to take over as president of the University of the Philippines and concurrently Secretary of Education, in 1964, he noticed that all the rest rooms and halls in the education department on Arroceros Street were dirty and littered.

"Don't we have janitors?" he asked. The employee list carried the names of 130 people as porters and janitors. "Where are they?"

"They come once a month to pick up their checks," he was told.

In the foreign service, the officers abroad who took a fancy to the country where they were stationed could insist on staying if they had a powerful friend back home. "We could not recall over-staying service officers abroad," explained an undersecretary in the Department of Foreign Affairs. "We had people in choice spots like Paris or Rome or London who had been there ten, fifteen years instead of the prescribed four-year tour of duty, and there was nothing we could do about it. If the Secretary tried to recall them, a senator or congressman would come and tell him not to. If he persisted, they would threaten to slash his budget."

The Secretary of Defense also found that he could not so much as order the removal of one soldier from a province without "having to contend with the mayor, the governor, and the congressman."

The arrogance and vindictiveness of the politicos was an especial nuisance to cabinet members trying to get their job done. "They would come any time they wished, in your office or house," recalled Romulo, who was Secretary of Education, then Secretary of Foreign Affairs in the Marcos cabinet, "without an appointment, and barge in with their bodyguards. Once when I arrived at my office there was a British diplomat who had an appointment at ten waiting to see me, and a senator and his three bodyguards. When I received the Ambassador first, the senator accused me of putting him ahead 'because he's a white man.' When they found out I was an early riser, they would appear at my house, when I was shaving, at six or 6:30 in the morning—then complain if I didn't offer them and their men breakfast."

To the constant discomfort of the administration, the majority of newspapers as well as radio and television stations were part of the commercial empires owned by the oligarchies—and in any tiff between government and the reigning families, it was the latter who controlled the communications media. At at time when President Marcos refused to replace a high-ranking military officer who happened to have offended the wife of the publisher of a Manila newspaper, at the request of her husband (the personal vendetta, the President claimed, had no bearing on the man's efficiency in his job), the newspaper promptly launched a hate campaign against both the President and Mrs. Marcos—and even succeeded in stirring up so much suspicion about the financing of Mrs. Marcos' pet project, Manila's Cultural Center, that she was taken to court to answer the charges (which proved false).

Politics had not only become "a business" in the Philippines, but it had begun to assume the complexion of an outlaw business—with politicians maintaining their power by such strong-arm tactics as the maintenance of private armies, bodyguards, and sophisticated weaponry.

"As Secretary of National Defense, I kept denying there were private armies because it was very embarrassing for me not to be able to contend with them," admits Secretary Enrile, "but for me to fight them with the resources I had available at that time and the array of formidable opponents I had in Congress would have been foolhardy and futile. They could have cut off my budget, asked my people not to follow me. I would have ended up accomplishing nothing and having a lot of enemies."

The usual political opposition to the President during Marcos's first administration took on an increasingly deadly hue as the President pressed for economic and social reform. The American congressional sport of "kick the President" was translated into a Philippine version of "kill the President." Unlike the fame-seeking lone assassin that characterized many of the attempts on the lives of American presidents, the assassination efforts at Marcos were coolly professional and politically motivated. In the conspiracy of 1969 (which sworn statements indicate can be traced to the door of a former cabinet member and was financed by the same group who had been actively involved in getting both Presidents Quirino and Macapagal out of office before they could achieve reforms) one of the plans involved an attempt to shoot the President with a rifle equipped with a telescopic sight while he was playing golf (as the Philippines's wartime collaboration president, Laurel, had been shot, and wounded, by patriot guerrillas during the Japanese occupation). An alternate plan called for the detonating of a bomb placed on the presidential yacht. Both efforts were foiled by the President's security, but the plot was uncovered and the assassins were found to be American hired guns who had previously been employed by American unions and Mafia leaders. (Although they were Americans no link has been established between the CIA and the Philippine conspiracy. It was, in fact, due to the cooperation of the U.S. embassy in Manila that the Philippine government was able to finger one of the conspirators.)

It was also not unusual for the President's opponents in Congress to support subversives, supplying them with money, food, and even arms, to make trouble for the administration. One of the government's charges against former Tarlac Senator Benigno S. Aquino, Jr. (whose case was recently brought to military court and then postponed for further review after Aquino refused to accept the jurisdiction of the military court and dismissed his lawyers) was of paying 15,000 pesos to support demonstrations staged before Congress, Malacanang Palace, and the U.S. embassy in April 1969.

In order to whip up anti-United States sentiment, and not incidentally embarrass the President in his friendly relations with the United States, Senator Aquino (who intended to run against Marcos for the presidency two years later) also charged that the United States had nuclear weapons on Philippine soil, and that atomic weapons had been discovered at Clark Air Force Base and Subic Bay. To support this claim Aquino is reported to have paid two American sergeants to appear before a congressional committee and testify that they personally observed nuclear weapons at these sites.

When a friend chided Aquino about the gravity of

such political mischief, saying, "I am positive there aren't any nuclear weapons there, and I think you are, too," Aquino is said to have responded airily, "All's fair in love and politics!"—thus echoing the same lighthearted cynicism of the land baron who told *Look* editorial writer John Hughes in 1968, "You don't understand the name of the game [here]. In the Philippines, if you're rich you don't stop. You just keep on going!"

In the face of such political anarchy, martial law itself had been a possibility long before Marcos chose to exercise it. As early as 1970, following the stoning of the presidential car and the attack on the palace, Major General Rafael Ileto, the West Point-trained Vice Chief of Staff, speaking for the generals, urged the President to declare martial law. The country, Ileto pointed out, was clearly in a state of anarchy which the military was powerless, under the present system, to quell. Following the storming of the palace gates the generals had all unanimously agreed to ask that martial law be declared. "We can establish peace and order if you'll do it," General Ileto advised the President. "But without that we cannot." He urged the President to proceed without fear of a military coup. "We will get the situation under control," he promised Marcos, "and then we will withdraw. We are not political men. We have no political ambitions."

The President was fortunate in the caliber of the military men around him. The Philippine armed forces and constabulary, while quite small (there are only 60,000 in all, as compared with Taiwan's 600,000), are known for their high level of training and discipline. The generals —several, like Ileto, West Point men—are top-level career soldiers of such stature that it is not unusual for them to "retire" to the ambassadorial circuit. The former Chief of Staff, General Yan, for example, is now the Philippine ambassador to Thailand.

Marcos chose to hold off, however, for another two years, in the hope of being able to implement the "social revolution" he envisioned within the existing system—especially after the ratification of the new constitution which was being drawn up.

It is clear to any serious Marcos-watchers, from his speeches and his book *(Today's Revolution: Democracy)*, that he had in mind a full-scale restructuring of society all along—and that he saw himself as its leader. In 1949 when, at the age of thirty-two, he became the youngest member of Congress, the ex-guerrilla war hero (Marcos was the most decorated for bravery of any Filipino in World War II) told his constituents in his hometown of Batac in Ilocos Norte:

"If you are electing me just to get my services as a congressman for the pittance of P7,500 [around $3,750] a year, don't vote for me at all. This is only the first step. Elect me now . . . and I pledge you an Ilocano president in twenty years [he made it in fifteen] and with the realization of the dreams we have all fought a war to win. . . ."

Along with many of those who demonstrated against him, the President saw revolution as the only means of righting the age-old wrongs that plagued the country. In a speech before a youth group in 1969, Marcos said, ". . . the old ways must go; the old politics, the old economics, the old social concepts—all of which have sustained the establishment and perpetuated the inequities of the past. . . .

"Philippine political life," he noted, "has been domi-nated by vested interests of factions, the selfish loyalties of clans . . . the power of the few."

He saw the youth as demanding "the substance of true politics . . . the art of managing men, material and resources for the growth and happiness of a nation."

During an otherwise unspectacular first term in office, Marcos had quietly assembled a task force of able, apolitical specialists in his cabinet, the "technocrats" needed to carry out his vision of a restructured society. Drawn from the private sector, the members of the President's "brain trust" were predominantly young Harvard-trained educators serving on the faculty of the University of the Philippines. They were not personal friends of the President, nor even political allies, but simply the ablest men in their respective fields. There was the young financial wizard Cesar Virata, who left his twin posts as college professor and financial advisor to major Manila companies to become Marcos's Secretary of Finance. Rangy, handsome Juan "Johnny" Enrile, who came in first as Undersecretary of Finance and then moved over to direct the Department of Defense, had been one of the Philippines's best-known tax and corpora-tion lawyers. Scholarly, banjo-eyed Gerardo Sicat was the University of the Philippines's leading economist before he assumed directorship of the National Economic Development Administration. Vicente Paterno had made his mark as a vigorous young industrialist and executive vice-president of the Manila Electric Company when he came in to head the government's Board of Investments. Sharp-tongued, impish columnist Francisco Tatad, whose editorial barbs had not spared Marcos himself, was called in at thirty-two to become the country's youngest Secretary of Public Information. None of these men (all younger than the fifty-year-old President) was Marcos's close friend or political buddy. "I didn't know the President very well when he offered me this job—and I still don't," Tatad said crisply. "And I'll bet the other cabinet members will tell you the same thing."

Perhaps because of their innocence of political hassle, men like former professors Sicat and Virata were frustrated by the congressional stalemate they encountered. "You'd come up with exciting plans and ideas," Sicat, a prematurely balding, serious man, recalled soberly, "and you were able to convince the President and the rest of the cabinet—and then Congress would sit on them. Each session you'd spend time preparing for the congressional hearings, appearing at the hearings—and then you'd see Congress adjourn with nothing done. It was very disappointing, very discouraging."

Cesar Virata—bushy crew-cut and whimsical—described how Congress functioned—or, more correctly, failed to. "If the President was pushing a good law, the politicians went to work on him, getting maximum leverage out of him. They would block the law or bill until they had worn him down to agree to every concession and appointment they wanted."

"It takes a great deal of effort," Virata added thoughtfully. "We appeared in Congress for so many hearings, in both the Senate and the House, on the same subject. Yet when Congress would adjourn, nothing had happened. Every year the same thing over again—all that time wasted and not one thing to show for it!"

Virata gave as an example the efforts of the Marcos administration to get a service contract to encourage foreign investment in oil exploration—which could have been an enormous shot in the arm to the laggard Philippine economy, bringing in both potential income and much-needed employment:

"I started working on that in 1968. I was Chairman of the Board of Investments. We had very little money in the agency, so I appealed to the National Science Development Board to contribute and we got enough to hire an oil consultant from the United States who made a report on how we should proceed to open up the industry. We prepared a bill and submitted it to Congress in 1969. It was immediately opposed by one of the 'nationalists' whose line was, 'If we allow the big boys in, the Philippines will be swallowed.'

"Then the people at the Stock Exchange got into the act. Each of them had a little oil company (on paper, anyway), and they made money trading shares back and forth. They formed a lobby in the Senate and the House.

"We'd get hearings, but no action.

"We appeared each year—1969, 1970, 1971—and nothing was ever done. Finally, in 1972, it passed the House, but under our bicameral system the Senate could pass a different sort of bill and you didn't know whether you were getting a camel or a horse. . . ."

(In September 1972, after martial law was declared, Virata updated the original proposal; it was approved by presidential decree and the first service contract was awarded in December 1972. September 1973 saw the signing of the largest service contract ever made by the Philippine government with an international oil conglomerate, which brought in a drilling rig the following week for offshore exploration in the Sulu Sea area, only miles from the lucrative Borneo strike.)

With all of its programs for economic and social development blocked at every turn, the early Marcos government suffered from a crisis of confidence both nationally and internationally. The Philippine National Bank was on the verge of bankruptcy. The Insurance Commission was so notoriously corrupt that no foreign insurer would accept an insurance policy written by a local company. The Bureau of Customs could not control the ports of Manila and smuggling was so well organized—and protected by the powerful figures involved, some of them members of Congress—that the government was losing an estimated 200 million pesos a year in revenues. (The Manila *Times* cynically suggested in 1968 that one way to reduce losses from smuggling was to bar the Manila city police from the waterfront!)

It was difficult to see, outside the inner circle of the administration itself, that Marcos was any more serious about his proposed reforms than any other politician had been. The President, after all, was a politican, too—and typically Filipino in that he had facilely switched from one party to another. He had had to accept the support of powerful political blocs to get into office. His reelection had been one of the most expensive and bitterest of campaigns marked by violence and dirty tricks on both sides. When he spoke of tax reform, or putting teeth into the long overdue agrarian reform program, or cleaning up corruption in the Department of Finance, it all sounded like another campaign speech.

Having earned the reputation for being the "most violent city in the Orient," noted for corruption of city and government officials, daily muggings and kidnappings, and strident nationalism ("Yankee go home"), Manila was not attracting foreign capital in the form of either tourists or investors. "You couldn't get foreign capital in here," explained Enrique Santamaria, the Spanish-born president of the Manila Stock Exchange. "They were frightened off by all the violence, all those guns. . . . I was in Barcelona when I heard martial law had been declared and I booked the next flight home. My Spanish friends couldn't understand it. 'You're going back—*now?*' But I was in a hurry to get back. I knew once we had peace and order things would begin to move."

One of the first clues as to just how serious the President was about a reform program showed up during his first term when he directed an official crackdown on smuggling, ordered the prosecution of smugglers, and fired 107 officials in the Bureau of Customs known to be involved with smugglers. In his first State of the Union message as President, Marcos had called attention to "that cancerous evil that has wreaked havoc on our economy and weakened the moral fiber of our people." Smuggling was so accepted that it was a status symbol to smoke only "blue seal" (untaxed) cigarettes and matrons flocked regularly to buy yard goods smuggled from Hong Kong rather than support local textile businesses. High-placed citizens in business and politics were known smugglers, and it was such a well-entrenched form of acquiring wealth that when the Departments of Justice and Defense actually did begin to enforce the revenue laws the constabulary lost more men than they had in armed combat against the Communists in central Luzon.

One of the most powerful congressmen, Senator Ganzon, tried to interfere with the customs crackdown, and when acting Undersecretary of Justice Enrile resisted him the senator moved to stop Enrile's confirmation. With the President's backing, however, Enrile fought back. Let him tell it:

"You know what I did? He [Ganzon] was controlling all of the city of Iloilo because he had appointed all the prosecution people there; nine of them. I fired all nine, and then prosecuted his own nephew who was a killer. . . . The Senate President, Puyat, called me to his office and asked me to relent on Ganzon. But I refused and the President backed me.

"We had to show the people we meant business," explained Enrile, "but it was not easy. . . . You could file all the charges, and then when they reached the courts, they would get acquitted."

As Secretary of Justice, Enrile did succeed in prosecuting some of the "untouchables," including Estrella, the former mayor of Makati, Manila's wealthiest suburb, and the son of a Speaker of the House.

But what few reforms and criminal indictments could be implemented were too little and too late. By 1970 the Philippines contained all the elements for a bloody revolution: an unemployment crisis; an economic crisis; and a mounting revolutionary mood. "We are sitting on top of a social volcano," Marcos warned, "and it may explode at any time."

The boiling point was being reached by the increasing numbers of young and poor—many of them with educations and high expectations—whose demands were unmet. While the top ten percent who controlled the wealth got richer each year, only one percent of the populace, including the millionaires and billionaires, earned $5,000 or more per year.

The Papal Nuncio in Manila, who had served in Bolivia,

likened the situation in the Philippines to that of Cuba before Fidel Castro.

When Marcos finally did move, in September 1972, it was as much to break the political stranglehold which choked the economic and social life of the country as it was against the apparent danger posed by demonstrators and activists, and the Communist and Muslim insurgents. The reasons that had led the young demonstrators to protest, and the landless peasants to join an alien ideology, were actually problems which the President understood very well and sympathized with. He had stated, over and again, that the country must change, that the society must be restructured, else it faced dissolution. He had warned that the government must be given a chance to alter the age-old inequities, and that vested interest must relax its stranglehold if the nation was to survive. But his warnings had been ignored.

Now he chose to put himself and his "social revolution" on the line. By rendering his enemies weaponless, he took sole responsibility for his program. There would be no one else to blame if it failed. When Marcos declared martial law even his detractors admitted it was an act of courage. The buck at long last had stopped at the door marked Office of the President. Marcos would lead his country to its long overdue destiny or he would go down with it.

That Marcos had no interest in killing or injuring the demonstrators—most of whom were college age—is evidenced by the Defense Department's orders, which were to "round up all troublemakers. *Immobilize them and avoid bloodshed.*"

When the military moved, at one o'clock on the morning of September 23, it moved swiftly and without incident, so far as the public was concerned. What injuries were sustained that night were sustained by the military, when three marines were mistakenly fired upon and injured by the militant Iglesia Ni Kristo (Church of Christ) religious group.

General Ileto had not misled the President about the nonpolitical role the military would play if martial law was declared. They established peace and order and withdrew. There was no attempt at a military coup. The military operation was under the direction of Marcos's civilian Secretary of Defense Enrile. The actual task of implementing peace and order fell on the slender shoulders of small, mild-mannered Brigadier General Fidel Ramos, Chief of the Philippine constabulary, a soft-spoken West Pointer who looks as though he'd be more comfortable conducting a class in comparative lit than running a military mop-up drive.

Somewhat to the surprise of the government officials involved, the politicians' private armies surrendered without a struggle. Apparently caught off-guard by the swiftness of the military action, they had no time to regroup and the constabulary was able to disarm all of them peaceably. The government officials were also surprised to find that the private armies numbered as high as one thousand men. But what emerged as an even more staggering fact was the amount of private firearms at large. "Can you imagine," said Secretary Enrile in an awed tone, "a country the size of the Philippines having from 500,000 to 800,000 firearms in the hands of its population? Five hundred thousand of them unlicensed? It is incredible. Our estimate was maybe 150,000. . . ."

"It was beyond our wildest dreams," agreed General Ramos. By July 1973 the Philippine constabulary had collected over half a million (523,449) unauthorized weapons—the largest number ever surrendered by any nation in history.

The haul included highly sophisticated arms—foreign-made high-powered automatic rifles and machine guns. One politician's estate yielded, in addition to handarms, two tanks. In a Communist cell in Bulacan, the constabulary picked up 300 assault rifles, rocket launchers, land mines, and grenades. Senator Aquino's personal cache of illegal firearms included, in addition to assorted rifles, a supply of hand grenades, 3 machine guns, and 4,470 rounds of ammunition.

In the initial military action, all known dissidents, activists, demonstrators, corrupt government officials, and citizens involved in what the government considered subversive groups or activities were rounded up—fifteen thousand in all across the country. In the Manila area the detainees were placed in Fort Bonifacio, Camp Crame, and Camp Aguinaldo.

An armed confrontation had been avoided. And time had been gained by the administration to convince its citizenry, detainees along with the rest, that this time the government meant business, that for once it was listening to the age-old protests. Within days following the initial mop-up operations, the long and arduous process of individual review and release of detainees began. (By September 1973 over nine thousand had been released.)

Now, with all its enemies disarmed or locked up, it was up to the Marcos administration to prove that its political "promises, promises" was more than the "title of a song," as one cynical young Filipino had called them. There was no more excuse for lack of national progress.

At long last the Philippine government was free to represent the interests and needs of the majority—those ninety percent of previously nonprivileged citizens.

Just who were these masses of forty million Filipinos, anyway? Where had they come from?

3

Who Are the Filipinos Anyway?

Whether the average American cares or not, it is to our interest to learn who the inhabitants of our former colony are—if only for the obvious pragmatic reason that today the Philippines ranks fifteenth among the nations of the world in population, which means there are already nearly as many Filipinos as there are, say, Italians, or French. The country is also, oddly enough, considering its Pacific setting and Spanish colonial history, the third largest English-speaking country in the world (next only to the United States and Great Britain—a spot that logically should be held by Canada, Australia, or New Zealand which are faulted in the first case by the large French-speaking population, and in the latter two by the paucity of population). The Philippines also boasts one of the highest literacy rates in Asia—second only to Japan—so that it offers American or British business interests its best equipped manpower for Asian enterprise.

On a social level, which must also be reckoned with, Filipinos are the most westernized and cosmopolitan of

Asians and they have persistently out-married (both Europeans and Americans) at a higher rate than other Asians. (One of the chauvinist Philippine jokes has to do with differentiating Filipinos from Chinese, Japanese, Koreans, Indonesians, Thais, and the rest of their Asian brothers, concluding that, while Japanese have the squattest bodies, Indonesians are the handsomest, Chinese look the most intellectual, etc., the Filipinos are easy to identify because they are the "sexiest.")

Certainly, by western standards, Filipinos are among the easiest to know of all Asians—they seem deceptively familiar, with their oddly accented but easily understood English, their western dress, Rotary Clubs, Jaycees, and Coca-Cola. Their music, religion, social manners are so comfortable that it often comes as a shock, on closer acquaintance, to find beneath the westernized facade, the Asian mystique alive and flourishing. Scratch the friendly surface, and you are still dealing with an Asian with Asiatic values (which finds western technology inferior to eastern humanism) and a slow, smoldering, but nonetheless fiery Asian pride, with its inherent longing for Asian identity free from western and superpower influence.

A bewildering and often quite beautiful physical mixture of all the bloodlines that have reached their shores (Malay, Chinese, Spanish, English, American; the 1973 Miss Universe, a granddaughter of President Roxas, has Malay, Spanish, Chinese, and American Negro ancestry), Filipinos are an adaptable people more openly hospitable to strangers, less insular than the Chinese or Japanese. Americans and British in Asia have always preferred being based in Manila to Tokyo or Hong Kong for the simple reason that the Japanese or Chinese, no matter how closely you deal with him, will seldom invite you to his home, while the Filipino not only welcomes, but fetes the stranger. The Spanish love for fiesta, superimposed on the openhanded Malay hospitality (the product of inexhaustible riches from the sea and land), has produced a country that, for one example, celebrates Christmas longer than any other nation in the world.

Filipinos seem, on first glance, somewhat like suntanned, almond-eyed Americans. They not only speak English, use the western alphabet and musical scale, and dress in western garb—but they also practice western religion. The only Christian nation in the Orient, nearly eighty-three percent of the country's population of forty million people is Catholic, with the remaining seventeen percent divided among Protestants and the non-Christian minorities, the largest of which, the Muslim Filipinos, represent about six and a half percent of the total population. Although the majority of Filipinos are from the same basic racial stock (southern Mongoloid), there are eighty different ethnic groups represented in the islands. Three of these, however, who number about the same percent as the Catholics and are, indeed, the same group—the Ilocanos, Tagalogs, and Visayans—from the central and northern sections of the country, dominate the social, economic, and political scene. The Muslims are concentrated in the southern island of Mindanao, and the other minority non-Christian tribes are scattered in isolated pockets throughout the islands, and are only now receiving official security for the lands they do occupy.

To the European or American, and to many wealthy Filipinos as well, the Philippines is Luzon—center of money power and government—far and away the heaviest populated and most developed section of the country.

The Visayas—the clutch of seven medium-sized islands occupying the central section of the Philippine archipelago —is second in development, containing several busy cities, primarily market centers for agricultural products from the area. To the south lies the large island of Mindanao which, despite its vast agricultural and mineral resources, has remained relatively neglected until recently.

Looking down from the air upon the 7,000-odd islands that form the Philippine archipelago, one realizes it would still be possible to live out one's days in the Philippines in utter isolation. There is little in the form of connecting links between the islands (only this year, 1973, the large islands of Samar and Leyte were joined by a bridge, which is one of the longest in southeast Asia) and much of the interior is uncharted jungle. The fact that a Stone Age tribe, the Tasadays, who still rub sticks to make fire and subsist on wild vegetables, fruits, and flowers which they hand-gather, was discovered only this past year in southern Mindanao is an indicator of the extent of uncharted interior that still exists in the islands, and offers a tantalizing glimpse of the self-sufficient existence possible in a warm, moist jungle climate with unpolluted streams and luxuriant vegetation.

The string of islands, which stretches over 1,000 miles from north to south in the center of the Pacific basin, lies only 15 miles off Borneo at the southern tip, and less than 150 miles from Taiwan at the north. Archeologically, the islands would seem to have been at some prehistoric time connected by a land bridge to the mainland of Asia, and it is thought that the islands' aborigines, the curious little pygmy Negritos who inhabit the highlands of northern Luzon, probably came overland via the land bridge from central Asia in the middle Pleistocene age, some 25,000 years ago.

Recent archeological findings indicate that the Philippines may well be one of the oldest inhabited sections of southeast Asia. The Tabon Caves, found in Palawan in 1962, show habitation by man at least 50,000 years ago, which may quite possibly stretch back 250,000 years, judging by the animal fossils found there.

Although their civilization is among the world's oldest, Filipinos who travel abroad are apt to discover that the outside world—especially the western world—is but little aware of either their country or of them as people. In 1919, when Carlos P. Romulo went to the United States to take his master's degree in American literature at Columbia University, he found to his distress that from the moment he left Manila he was not only not recognized as a Filipino (he was assumed to be Chinese even in Hong Kong), but his country was known in only the vaguest of geographical terms. ("Part of Hawaii, isn't it?" "Somewhere near Australia?") One of his Columbia classmates, whose family had attended the St. Louis Exposition in 1904 and seen loin clad members of the Igorot tribe from the Philippines Mountain Province on display, asked Romulo solicitously if he didn't find wearing trousers for the first time "itchy" and uncomfortable.

A quarter of a century later, when Romulo was lecturing in America, the situation had scarcely improved. Sharing a platform with the British Labor Prime Minister Clement Attlee, who had succeeded Churchill in 1945, Romulo dedicated the first part of his speech in praise of Attlee because of Attlee's recognition of India's claim to independence (which had reversed Churchill's policy of

British colonialism in Asia). In response Attlee thanked
Romulo—but confessed that he did not know "just where"
the Philippines actually was, and added that Romulo was
the first FiliPIno he had ever met.

At the first International Boy Scout Jamboree attended
by Filipino Scouts in Hungary in 1933, the 7-boy Philippine delegation was discomfited to find that none of the
25,000 other boys from all over the world had ever heard
of their country. They were repeatedly asked if they were
Chinese or Japanese—which seemed to be the limit of
Asian nationalities known to the westerners. And when
they found their Hungarian hosts walking behind them,
staring and whispering, and asked them why they were
doing so, the Hungarians confessed that they were "looking for your tails. We heard that people from your part
of the world all have tails."

It often comes as a surprise to the westerner to discover
a Filipino with international scope, intellect, or social
sophistication, despite the fact that those Filipinos who
could afford it have been traveling and studying abroad
since the sixteenth century. The islands' national hero,
Dr. Jose Rizal, spent a third of his life in the capitals of
Europe and spoke twenty-two languages. Once, when the
fate of the Philippines was an issue before the United
States Congress, a congressman sympathetic to Philippine
desire for independence read one of Rizal's poems to
prove that the United States was not dealing with un-
lettered barbarians.

Such clichés have not faded with time as much as might
be supposed. That the insidious putdown of the Filipino
as a person to be reckoned with intellectually or culturally
still obtains was proved recently when Swedish sociologist
Gunnar Myrdal, upon meeting with Philippine writer

Adrian Cristobal in Europe, wrote to a Swedish friend in Manila that "the intelligence of Cristobal is beyond our wildest expectations"! Why, indeed, was Dr. Myrdal so surprised to find high intellect in these scattered Asian islands? Yet it is an attitude Filipinos have learned to expect from westerners who automatically assume the Philippine mind must be not only provincial but primitive.

In point of fact, Filipinos have always had the outward-seeking mentality of a seafaring people. Their Malay forefathers who arrived by ship from Indonesia and settled along the coast traded with neighboring Hong Kong and Singapore, and the ports have always been multilingual. After the Spanish invasion Filipinos served on the Spanish galleons that made the five-month voyage from Manila to Acapulco.

Favored Filipinos of the nineteenth century went to "mother" Spain in search of education or perhaps national identity. Filipinos studied, as did Dr. Rizal, in Madrid, London, Paris, Rome.

Like the Thais, Filipino families who can afford to do so traditionally send their children to European or American universities. And until the travel restriction imposed this past year under martial law, they spent their own vacation time and money on trips to Europe or the United States. This passion for travel is shown today by the fact that of all the limitations imposed by martial law the one which one hears the most discontent about is the travel ban. (An emergency measure introduced by the government to reverse the dollar drain.) A plan is now being considered which would ease the travel restrictions but levy a tax on travel and put a limitation on how much money could be taken abroad—a system which England found it necessary to impose long ago.

With an imbalance of education and employment which threw many educated Filipinos on a shrinking market at home, Filipino professionals—doctors, lawyers, engineers, nurses—have, in the past two decades, gone abroad to work. There are so many Filipino doctors and nurses in the United States today that it is said our national health services would collapse if they were all recalled home.

Like many Europeans who have found that their social and economic survival demands knowing the languages of the countries whose borders they share, Filipinos have found it essential to know the languages of the countries they deal with, with the result that the majority of Filipinos are excellent linguists. The various Filipino dialects are in themselves so difficult for foreigners that government officials have found they are useful as a code in conveying secret information internationally. (Presidents Quezon and Magsaysay talked to their "man in Washington," Ambassador Romulo, in Ilocano or Tagalog, for instance, with no fear that taps by the CIA or other interested parties would be able to unscramble what they were saying.)

By necessity Filipinos speak, in addition to their own regional dialect, the national language, Pilipino, which is the Tagalog dialect of Luzon where Manila is located. Spanish is still the polite social language of many upperclass families. And Filipinos rich and poor understand, and usually speak, English. (Even the provincial Filipinos who may be shy to speak it will nonetheless understand what is said in English.) In addition, Filipinos who work and travel abroad invariably command the language of the country they have spent time in. Filipino singers and musicians—who are in such demand in neighboring Taiwan, Hong Kong, Singapore, and Japan because they perform western music for American and European tourists—are apt to speak Chinese or Japanese. Many Filipino students and adults who got their schooling in Europe speak French.

Settled primarily by the Malays who came by boat from Malaysia and Indonesia, the early pre-Christian Philippines was regularly visited by both Arab and Chinese traders, and Chinese settlers began arriving in the fourteenth and fifteenth centuries, although the bulk of the Philippines's current Chinese population (300,000 people) came in a single decade, between 1886 and 1896, from a single province, Fukien. The upheaval responsible for that mass migration was the British Lipton Company's development of tea plantations in Ceylon, which snatched the world tea market away from Fukien. A densely populated province, Fukien was rendered destitute by the loss of a market for its principal product, and the young Chinese males emigrated en masse to support themselves and their families back home. Looking for work in Hong Kong, Taiwan, Singapore, and the Philippines, many of them settled in the Philippines and married Filipinas— which accounts for the many "Chinese mestizos" in the Philippine population. With their mothers' beauty and their fathers' financial wizardry, many of these Chinese mestizos became leaders in the Philippine financial and business community, and some, as Philippine nationals, became part of the landowning class. (The Chinese were hardworking and thrifty, and in so many instances were able to build up wealth from a standing start of a tiny shop or peddler status, through thrift and self-deprivation that they earned both the grudging admiration and some hostility from the less thrifty, more easygoing Malay Filipinos who dubbed them "the Jews of the Orient"—showing toward the Chinese the same sort of resentment of business success which accounted for some of the early United States anti-Semitism.)

The traders who made the most dramatic impact on the history and eventual social problems of the Philippines, however, were the Arabs. It is now estimated that if that first group of Spanish colonists, led from Mexico by Legaspi in 1565, had reached the Philippines fifty years later than they did they would have found the Philippines already totally converted to Islam—and the rest of Asia never would have experienced the anachronism of a western Christian neighbor in the Pacific (nor the Philippines have had to endure the tragic religious dichotomy of Christian brother pitched against Muslim brother which haunts the country to this day).

Islam, which had first been introduced into southern Sulu in the late fourteenth century by Arab missionaries and then spread throughout the large island of Mindanao, had, by the time the Spanish arrived, already reached north as far as Manila, in northern Luzon, which was a Muslim fortress and port. The Spanish Christians conquered the Muslims in Manila and drove them back south to Mindanao where they were to remain entrenched, fighting first the Spanish and then the Americans for the next four hundred years. The fierce and warlike Muslims never did, in fact, surrender to anyone and were thus never colonialized. Because of this they retain the only indigenous culture in dance, art, costume, that remains in the Philippines.

Although the Spanish systematically destroyed most aspects of the Malay culture (religion, dress, art, etc.), the Malay legacy survives in some of the more ingratiating elements of Filipino life and personality: it shows up in

food, in the fascinating array of rice dishes, the use of
suckling pig. Whether it can be laid to Malay alone, or
the mix of Malay-Spanish, it is not a cliché to say Filipinos have an edge on musical ability, since most Filipinos are able, at least passably, to play some instrument,
dance, and sing. They furnish musicians for the orchestras
of neighboring Asian countries, supplying ninety-five percent of the musicians in Hong Kong, for instance. The
openhanded there's-no-tomorrow Filipino hospitality is
certainly derivative of a race that never was hungry or
cold. The natural uncomplicated sexuality which has survived the strictures of the Catholic Church, nineteenth-
century Victorianism carried eastward by the British, and
English-style dress certainly must be credited to the easygoing Malay. The adaptibility to other people and cultures
also speaks of an island-hopping people rather than the
Spanish who can be withdrawn and insular. And no one
could accuse the Spanish, despite their romantic charm, of
possessing a national sense of humor. But this the Filipinos do have. It is so apparent that they are known,
within the Asian community, as the *only* Asians with a
sense of humor—despite the Chinese claim to a uniquely
delicate and dry humor all their own. But the Filipino
humor is lustier, more spontaneous, and more easily
shared. The recently appointed papal envoy to Manila,
Monsignor Bruno Torpigliani, found the Filipinos' bub-
bling spirits very much like the Italians': sunny and warm.

The early development of the Philippines was as much
dictated by the equable climate as anything else. The
Malays established individual settlements which apparently remained undisturbed by outside influence for long
periods of time. With warm weather the year round, they
needed no more than an easily constructed nipa hut made

of bamboo and thatched with palm leaves to ward off
the elements. The sources of food were plentiful: rivers,
lakes, and coastal waters provided fish and shellfish;
fertile ground produced sweet potatoes, rice, and corn.

The earliest political structure was based on the community or kinship group, named *barangay* after the type
of boats that had carried the original settlers from their
homes in Malaysia to the Philippines. Boatloads generally
consisted of an extended family group—the leader and
his family, his brothers, sisters, and their spouses and children, and the old folks.

These barangays tended to be economically self-sufficient. They raised enough to eat and wear, and there
was little incentive for travel to neighboring communities
or for the development of technology.

Their contact with other local communities was apt to
be limited and to offset the necessity of hostilities the
groups developed certain ritual courtesies. To this day
Filipinos are very apt to say what the stranger wants to
hear rather than give a direct or honest answer, so as to
avoid offending him. As other Oriental rituals for face-
saving, this has been much misunderstood by westerners
who automatically become suspicious and think the Filipino elaborate politeness is devious and signifies that the
person cannot be trusted.

Today kinship is carried further in the Philippine social
order than in almost any other country—with the in-laws
of a family and their families considered as relatives.
The parents of a son, for instance, are considered related
to the sisters or brothers of the girl that their son marries,
and are expected to observe birthdays, anniversaries, etc.,
and offer appropriate gifts and favors. A sometimes de-
lightful antidote to the loneliness of American nuclear

family life, the demands of this extended kinship can prove a nuisance for anyone who prefers privacy, or holds a position of power. The head of the clan is open to constant importuning for patronage, letters of recommendation, political or business pressure on behalf of each member of his extended family. A person of celebrity or power, even when there is no kinship status, is often called upon, by the thinnest claims of family friendship, to sponsor weddings, funerals, christenings, and provide not only the weight of his physical presence but also substantial gifts.

The Malay leaders of clans enjoyed the responsibilities and obligations of head-of-clan status as well as the power. When the Spanish arrived in the sixteenth century, they found this patriarchal social structure already well established. Each community of kinsmen was led by a headman, or *datu*, who dispensed favors, patronage, judgment, acting as father, judge, and king of his near-to-distant relatives. The Spanish opportunistically sought out these community leaders and made them their tax collectors, government agents, etc., to take advantage of an already established social structure.

It was this structure which provided the Philippines with its two-class society: the patriarch-cum-landowners and the mass of ordinary citizens. The leader group, who also were to become the educated class, naturally gravitated to political office when it became available to native Filipinos.

The average man, as Rizal makes poignantly clear in his Dumas-like nineteenth-century romances, *Noli me Tangere* and *Filibusterismo*, which in their fashion played as powerful a role in the history of the Philippines as *Uncle Tom's Cabin* did in America, was defenseless unless he had a protector, a godfather, to fight his battles for him. "For it is well known in the Philippines that one needed patrons and protectors for everything from christening until death," Rizal wrote in the *Fili* as his second novel is called, "whether it was to secure a passport or to establish an industry or to obtain justice."

Historian Arnold Toynbee has said that a country's history cannot be told only in terms of its politics, economics, arts, and battles, but it must also be told in terms of its religions. Certainly the Philippines, the only Christian country in Asia, cannot begin to be understood without taking due observance of the influence of Catholicism on the country: how and when the Church arrived, how it has been modified to suit Malay tastes, and what it means to the Filipino, how it influences and alters his political and social progress.

Unlike much of the Orient with its ancient temples, the early Philippines had no churches. In its pre-Spanish Catholic, pre-Arab Muslim days, the Philippine religion was a form of animism, and to this day a wide variety of mythological creatures survive, especially in the rural areas; a cast of characters which includes demons, dragons, dwarfs, elves, ghouls, giants—with both good and evil characteristics—to which the peasants ascribe their physical ailments, the natural phenomena of eclipses and typhoons, and the vagaries of nature which influence the harvests. The dwarfs, who own the land, can be mollified by periodic offerings and can be foiled or frightened off by vinegar, garlic, and salt—which are also, incidentally, the predominant flavors in Filipino cookery.

Over this world of exotic animals and spirits, which are features of the natural environment, there was one Su-

Dr. José Rizal, the Philippine national hero who was
martyred by the Spaniards

Old Manila during the Spanish regime

(above) The Leyte Landing, when General Mac-Arthur (in foreground, followed by General Carlos P. Romulo) fulfilled his promise to return and liberate the Philippines

(below) The ruins of Intramuros, the walled inner city of Manila built by the Spaniards

The Leyte Landing

(on facing page) Emilio Aguinaldo, a general at eighteen, fought the Spaniards and then the Americans in the Philippine war for independence. He was the Republic's first President.

A skyline view of downtown Manila today

preme Being (*Bathala*), although the Malays found no need to build him a house. His existence, however, plus a shared belief in an afterlife, made Catholic proselytizing especially easy.

Magellan, who discovered the Philippines in 1521 on his historic voyage to prove the earth was round, actually had little to do with its colonization. Landing at Cebu, in the central Visayas, after an initial success converting to Christianity the local *datu* and his wife, Magellan made the mistake of tangling with another Malay chief, and managed to get himself killed. The chief, Lapu-Lapu, whose name means little to non-Filipinos beyond being the same as that of an edible fish, is a hero at home because he was the first Filipino to repulse the invasion of the white western world.

Magellan, however, had managed to plant the cross on Philippine soil before his death, and the survivors of the fateful voyage eventually reached their homeland, Spain, and spread the word of the riches for the taking in Asia. One of the five expeditions sent to retrace Magellan's course did reach the Philippines, a band of Spanish conquistadores under the command of Miguel de Legaspi. More diplomatic than his predecessor, Legaspi ingratiated himself with the local *datus* and was able to subdue the natives with a minimum of bloodshed, and take the country in the name of the king of Spain in 1565. (A nationalist movement a year ago lobbied to change the name of the Philippines, which was named for the Spanish king, to a Malay name, but was voted down on the theory that the country had had enough trouble getting the world to learn the old name without confusing it with a new one!)

Legaspi's secret weapon, which was more important in the long run than the firearms that frightened and subdued the natives, was the group of six friars whom he carried along with him from Spain to the Philippines.

Starting from their first settlement in Cebu, the Spaniards began an island-to-island conversion until they reached Manila. A thriving Muslim port, Manila was also a strong fortress. After bitter fighting, the Muslim chieftain, Rajah Soliman, finally surrendered, and Legaspi "founded" Manila as the capital of the Spanish Philippines.

There the Spaniards built their own fortress, a walled city, the Intramuros, with seven bridges spanning a moat, which were pulled up each night (it was here that General Douglas MacArthur had his office before the Japanese took Manila. Most of Intramuros was destroyed by Allied bombing in World War II), and Fort Santiago, which was later used by the Japanese as a prison camp.

When the Spanish took control of the country, they resettled the natives into "towns," for the purpose of government, which were built around a parish church and town hall in the plaza, with the residential areas laid out in a regular grid pattern from the central plaza. Friars held the reins of local government as well as churchly duties. The former leaders of the barangays were made the administrative officials of the colonial local regime, charged with the collection of taxes and the enforcement of labor. This combination of forced tribute and forced labor supported the Spanish colonials until they lost the islands at the end of the nineteenth century. The Spanish themselves were a nonproductive population of priests, soldiers, officials, and their families congregating mainly in Manila.

In its nearly four centuries of rule, Spain did little or nothing to develop the economy of the islands. The principal impact of their presence (the Spanish never numbered more than five thousand at one time) was religious. Within one century after they took the Philippines, the majority of Filipinos had been converted to Roman Catholicism—with the notable exception of the proud and warlike Muslims in the south.

Because of Spanish interest in trade, the Philippines developed in a different direction from the rest of southeast Asia. The islands were put under the administration of the Viceroy of Mexico, and Spanish ships began plying the route between Manila and Acapulco.

For two and a half centuries the Spanish colonials lived off this lucrative galleon trade between the Philippines and Mexico, congregating within their walled inner city in the port of Manila, neglecting the rest of the country, which was ruled and managed at the whim of the friars. The port of Manila provided the Spanish entrepreneurs with a way station between the Orient, with its treasure-house of silks and porcelain and spices, and Mexico and Spain. The Manila galleons, loaded (and often, to their later regret, overloaded) in Manila, sailed to Acapulco where the rich cargo was off-loaded onto mules, and thence overland to the Spanish capital at Mexico City, or to the port of Vera Cruz, and from there shipped to Spain.

Embarrassed by the charge of abuses of native labor in the Americas (and with the death of thousands of South American Indians on their national conscience), the Spanish crown prohibited mining operations in the Philippines, and in the beginning even prohibited the residence of Spanish nationals in the provinces, where encounter between the two cultures was limited to the "natives" and the church. Although this prohibition later was revoked, the tendency remained for the Spaniards to concentrate in Manila, leaving the provinces to the priests. As native Filipinos were to comment somewhat bitterly, the trip from Spain to Manila transformed every Spaniard into a nobleman. It was up to the "natives" not only to pay tribute and provide services for these noblemen, but also to raise enough food to feed them. It was not until the late eighteenth century that the Spanish showed a belated interest in what was basically an agricultural land, and turned their attention to the development of sugar and hemp plantations. Prior to that the friars had exacted "rentals" from the farmers who tilled the land, although legally the friars had no rights to own land. In the bitter portraits of the friars in action that we find in Rizal's fictional accounts, the usual practice was to wait until a farmer had developed land and it was temptingly productive, and then move in, claim it for the Church, and exact rentals. The rentals then went up ladderlike as the productivity increased.

Rizal gives us a portrait of the Spanish friars that is almost unrelieved in its lechery, villainy, cruelty, and avarice. At its kindest, the characterization is merely fatuous. The novelist accuses the friars of keeping the Filipino people ignorant deliberately, of exploiting them economically and sexually, and profiting from them.

It was Rizal's belief that the Philippines deteriorated badly under Spanish rule. It had been a society of freemen organized on the basis of kinship. Filipinos, before the Spanish arrived, were shipbuilders, exporters of silk and cotton, gold miners. The ancient Filipinos had their own alphabet and language. Under the four centuries of Spanish rule—and deliberate destruction of the Malay culture—the Filipinos lost the art of building ships, they abandoned their gold mines, they became illiterate and uneducated. Whole groups were decimated when the Spanish used them as soldiers, sailors, and galley slaves for their expeditions into Asia. The Spanish also forced the Christian Filipinos to fight the Muslim Filipinos in the south, so that many were killed by their own Muslim brothers.

The Spanish also introduced racism to the islands, by prescribing the lighter-skinned Spaniards superior to the darker Malays, with the result that the mestizos (the Malays who had Spanish blood) became the elite of succeeding generations. Much of the Spanish blood was supplied by the friars, who were often the only Spaniards dealing with the people in the provinces. Many mestizo families trace their lineage to particular Spanish friars serving in their towns or villages. The country's first president, Manuel Quezon, was said to be the light-skinned son of a friar.

Worst, perhaps, of the Spanish crimes against the Filipino, according to Rizal, was the decimation of the Malay pride. Without justice, Filipinos were reduced to begging or fawning to survive (if they resisted, as the heroes of his novels did, they were persecuted and killed, as Rizal himself eventually was).

To make sure that the natives could be easily differentiated from the "gentlemen," the Spanish forced all the Filipino men to wear sheer shirts made of native material (the now-popular Filipino dress shirt, *barong tagalog*). The see-through shirts also made it impossible for a native to hide a weapon. As a gesture to the development of national pride, President Magsaysay started a precedent for Filipino presidents always to appear in *barong*, which has been followed by subsequent presidents.

Despite the alacrity with which Filipinos embraced Catholicism, they were never quiescent under Spanish rule, and there was smoldering discontent and bitterness against the domination of Spain throughout the colonial period, which erupted into more than a hundred revolts. Finally, in 1896, the rebellion emerged into a full-scale revolution.

Although Rizal himself did not believe in bloody revolution ("reforms," he wrote in his Manifesto just prior to his execution in 1896, "if they are to bear fruit, must come from above . . ."), he was its inspiration in that he verbalized the Filipino spirit and its growing hopelessness under Spanish rule. In his own person, Rizal symbolized much of the Filipino national character; in addition to his dual careers as physician and novelist, Rizal was noted for his talents at languages, poetry, music, art, and love. He also set the pattern for out-marriage to Europeans by marrying his Irish sweetheart in his prison cell before his execution.

Comparing the Filipino to the Spanish temperament, Rizal once likened them to their national animals: the carabao and the bull. The Spanish bull is brave, fearless, obstinate. The Filipino carabao is a more peaceful animal, more patient and harder to excite. But once aroused, it struggles to the death.

The long-suffering patience of the Christian Filipinos came to an abrupt end in 1896 when, as a man, they massed against the Spanish. (The Muslims in the south, who had never yielded to Spanish domination, did not find the Christian Filipinos' revolution relevant to their position and took no part in it.)

The first nationalist revolution in Asia, the Philippine revolution was not a class war, but the political expression of a nation against the absolute authority of its rulers. Led initially by the young patriot, Andres Bonifacio, the revolt was carried to a surprisingly successful conclusion by General Emilio Aguinaldo, who managed to beat back the Spanish forces from the shores of his country (the superior forces of the Spanish were diverted by the set-to with the United States in Cuba) and declare the Philippines a republic only to have the revolution stolen from him by the United States, in the name of friendly assistance against the mutual enemy, Spain.

What both Spain, and subsequently America, failed to understand about the Filipino people was their very real revolutionary spirit, their honest hunger for independence.

4

A Very Special
Relationship

Few are apt to recall—except Filipinos themselves—that
the Philippines actually was an independent republic for
a few brief years between its victory over the Spanish
and its take-over by the United States, while the American president, McKinley, paced the White House floor
and struggled with his conscience at night and with
Congress during the day.* No one in Washington—not
even the president himself—knew precisely where the
Philippines was nor who Filipinos were, but in the end
the conclusion was that America would be doing right
by her "little brown brothers" if she would adopt them
and lead them along the road toward eventual self-
government "when they were ready."

The fact that the Philippines had its independence only
so long as the American President struggled with his soul
does not alter the fact of having achieved it. Just as

---

* The full and fascinating account of the acquisition of the Philippines
by the United States can be found in Margaret Leech's award-winning
In the Days of McKinley (Harpers, 1959) to which I am indebted for
some of the details that appear in this chapter.

Thailand can lay claim to having been an Asian country that was *never* colonized, so the Philippines can boast that it fought the first nationalist revolution in Asia and established the first democratic republic in Asia—which survived from 1898 to 1901, when America officially took over control of the islands. In 1946, when the Philippines did achieve its promised independence, it was the first former colony in Asia to win independence from western colonialism.

But the Philippines chooses to celebrate as its official Independence Day, not the date in 1946 when the United States finally fulfilled its promise to free the islands, but rather the date of June 12, when, in 1898, General Emilio Aguinaldo, as head of the Revolutionary Government, proclaimed the independence of the Philippines to the world, and he became the islands' first president. The Philippine flag is the flag of the Revolutionary Government, which was first unfurled at the house of General Aguinaldo in Kawit, Cavite: a sun with eight rays and three stars. The three stars represent the three major island groups: Luzon, the Visayas, and Mindanao; and the rays signify the eight provinces that declared revolution against Spain.

Filipinos are nothing if not ambivalent in their emotions about America. And one of the things that will remain unforgiven is that American officials declared the Philippine flag could not be publicly displayed—causing the patriots who had won their revolution against Spain to drape it in the privacy of their homes, above their beds. The Americans also outlawed political parties that favored independence, to discourage the development of a healthy nationalism which would have been the appropriate foundation for future self-government.

A voiceless pawn of the Spanish-American War (neither the United States nor Spain apparently felt the Philippines sufficiently developed to have any say in their own destiny and refused to allow the Filipino representative sent by the Revolutionary Government to sit in at the Treaty of Paris where the big powers decided the fate of the islands), the Philippines had revolted against Spain, unaware that Spain and the United States had clashed over Cuba. At the conference table in Paris in December 1898 Spain ceded the Philippines to the United States for $20 million, thus launching America on its initial try at the old European game of colonialism. The fact that the Philippines had won their fight against Spain and claimed themselves a republic, and no longer belonged to Spain, was a minor detail completely ignored by both powers.

Actually, this foray into colonialism was hardly a majority choice in the United States. The official American foreign policy at that time was isolationist. President McKinley had sought a peaceful diplomatic settlement with Spain over the Cuba issue—which was muffled by the zealous young Teddy Roosevelt's shout for American expansion and war with Spain. With the equally imperialistic Senator Cabot Lodge behind him, Roosevelt was able to whip up sufficient nationalistic frenzy and economic appetite to carry the day and lay hands on both Cuba and the Philippines. Roosevelt and Lodge correctly assayed that Spain's power was on the wane and saw the possibility of taking the Philippines as an opportunity for America to acquire a base in southeast Asia.

To justify (at least for the President, who was isolationist, pacifist, and religious) the United States aggression, it was carried out in both countries in a missionary spirit which was to color United States foreign policy toward its possessions and all developing countries (reaching its apogee under John Foster Dulles) for the next three-quarters of a century. Intervention, according to the official United States position, was a "duty" to the poor heathens who were in no condition for self-government.

Under the orders of Assistant Secretary of the Navy Roosevelt, Commodore George Dewey was dispatched to the Pacific to stand by in case war did break out between Spain and the United States in Cuba, so that he could seize Manila. When this particular warlike ploy was explained to President McKinley, the prospect of seizing the far-off island capital gave him pause. He admitted that he "could not have told where those darned islands were within two thousand miles."

When, indeed, the United States and Spain clashed, Commodore Dewey promptly set upon and defeated the Spanish fleet in Manila Bay—earning himself a role of national hero back home. Americans, oblivious of the islands' own little revolution, immediately assumed that "we" had taken the Philippines. Learned discussions were carried on in the American press as to what would be the most advantageous disposition of our new possession. Should we sell the islands to Germany or Japan? Should we try to run them ourselves? If so, should we take over all of the islands, or just the city of Manila? The Philippines was assumed to be ours "by right of conquest," and it was generally agreed that military rule would be absolute. McKinley, ever the good Christian, held out that the "natives" (whoever they were) should have their personal and property rights protected.

No one in America knew precisely what they had in the

Philippines. Heathens, they knew. And heathens in need of such American services as education, health, roads, and the like. America in general felt quite benign about what it would do for the heathen. And quite unaware of Filipino culture, nationalism, or independence.

Or of the Philippine independence army. The American forces who went in for a quick and peaceful take-over of the islands were unprepared for the strength, numbers, and military expertise of the rebel army. General Aguinaldo, they were shocked to discover, had at his command an army of thousands of men. Nervous word flew back to Washington from U.S. observers in Manila that the Philippine revolutionary army might not yield obedience to the United States army of occupation.

Admiral Dewey, who, while hardly a diplomat, took the trouble to meet the Philippine general, reported that Aguinaldo was in fact an admirable fellow, and that the Filipinos, rather than being hopeless heathens, were actually far superior in intelligence and more capable of self-government than the Cubans probably were. Dewey also promised Aguinaldo that if he would cooperate with American military strategy against Spain the Philippine Revolutionary Government would be recognized and the Philippines would have its freedom—a promise Dewey later did not recall having made.

General Aguinaldo, mistakenly believing in the American's promise of assistance, made an agreement with Admiral Dewey which enabled the American navy, backed by Filipino land forces, to hold Manila until United States ground troops arrived. Too late the Filipino general found that he had been tricked, and that his "liberators" were actually "imperialists." The Filipino army withdrew from Manila and set up a rebel government in Malolos, about fifty miles north.

To the dismay of Washington, Major General Thomas M. Anderson, who led the first expedition to Manila, reported that the Filipinos expected independence. Senator Lodge, giddy with the prospects of the new United States posture of imperialism, urged that the United States take the Philippines at once with military might if necessary. McKinley's Secretary of State, Judge William R. Day, dissented from this opinion. Judge Day pointed out that "taking" a country with millions of inhabitants seemed a questionable venture for a nation which prided itself on a government that rested on the consent of the governed.

The President, who was himself a very reluctant imperialist, joked that "if old Dewey had just sailed away when he smashed that Spanish fleet, what a lot of trouble he would have saved us!" Personally against the idea of colonizing the Philippines (or any country), McKinley spoke out against the "greed of conquest" and "criminal aggression." But the coalition of such fire-eating imperialists as Lodge and Roosevelt was too much for his and his old friend Day's quiet midwestern voices. After endless debate, pressure from both religious and commercial interests, and much soul-searching, McKinley finally capitulated, saying he "didn't want them . . . but there was no alternative." To rationalize a basically distasteful move, the President saw the take-over as a policy of enlightened colonization in which the United States would see it as its duty to take the backward islands and "educate them."

As Senator William Fulbright once noted, the United

States went to war for the purpose of "liberating Cuba
from Spanish tyranny," but after winning, "the U.S.
brought the liberated Cubans under an American protectorate and incidentally annexed the Philippines because,
according to President McKinley, the Lord told him it
was America's duty 'to educate the Filipinos and uplift
and civilize and Christianize them. . . .'"

That the Philippine "heathen" had a religion which
antedated Jamestown was a fact that apparently had
eluded the President. In an interview with the General Missionary Committee of the Methodist Episcopal
Church, he described the soul-searching that led to his
decision to take the Philippines: "I walked the floor of
the White House night after night until midnight, and
I am not ashamed to tell you gentlemen that I went
down on my knees and prayed Almighty God for light
and guidance more than one night. And one night late
it came to me this way—I don't know how it was but it
came . . . that there was nothing left for us to do but to
take them all and to educate the Filipinos and uplift
them and civilize and Christianize them and by God's
grace do the very best we could by them, as our fellow-
men for whom Christ also died. And then I went to bed,
and went to sleep and slept soundly and the next morning I sent for the chief engineer of the War Department
and I told him to put the Philippines on the map of the
United States, and there they are and there they will
stay while I am President!"

The fate of the Philippines was a major campaign issue
in 1900 when McKinley ran for reelection. Perennial
Democratic hopeful, William Jennings Bryan, attacked
incumbent President McKinley for being an imperialist
who had violated Filipinos' rights. "We dare not educate

the Filipinos," Bryan thundered, "lest they learn to read the Declaration of Independence and the Constitution of the United States."

Bryan, who probably knew little more about the Philippines than the Republicans, advocated making the islands a protectorate with the promise of eventual independence. McKinley, on the contrary, maintained that the protectorate idea would yield the government up to "guerrilla bands" who were the "murderers of our soldiers." The President's hope was to end military rule as quickly as possible and set up a civil administration.

The debate was so intense, however, that McKinley felt obligated to make a justification of his position on the Philippines two-thirds of his letter of acceptance to run again. In it he stated that he felt the United States' intervention was "unavoidable" and that the correct U.S. role should be to prepare Filipinos for self-government (not for economic gain but for "humanity and civilization"). He was very careful to take the position that Filipinos should be granted a sound educational system, civil service, and all the provisions of the Bill of Rights, except for trial by jury and the right to bear arms, and that a model colonial government should be created for them. McKinley's major error in his judgment of the Philippines was an assumption that the rebels, as Dewey had stated, represented only a minority of insurgents, and that the population actually consisted of a mass of impoverished and illiterate peasants, without a culture and without purpose, the majority of whom would welcome American rule.

The official rationale for taking the Philippines was the people's "political incapacity," and danger from other powers. A forerunner of the twenty-four-hour congressional or journalistic expert of a later era, Senator Albert Beveridge of Indiana made a quick trip to Manila and came back to report to the folks back home and to Congress that the Filipinos were "a stupid and indolent race" badly in need of the kindly guiding hand of America.

The colonial tendency in which many Americans joined the British, French, and Dutch was to downgrade the Asian as an inferior and primitive being, and perpetuate a "chink chink Chinaman" Asian stereotype, which was avidly reinforced by the popular press. The American film industry also added to this distortion with its stereotype Asians—cannibals, mysterious and devious opium kings, enigmatic Indians, deceitful dragon ladies.

The first western observers, starting with the Venetian Marco Polo, had found Asia a fascinating scene in contrast to Europe, and they had idealized it. But the later waves of western writers and observers who came to see for themselves couldn't see the culture for the dirt, and reacted by being disenchanted with everything Asian, writing in shocked detail about its obvious defects: mass poverty, disease, lack of respect for human life. The late-nineteenth-century immigration to the American west coast, the Chinese "coolies" who were indeed launderers and cooks, had made the Chinese a lowly and despised figure, which obtained in many western minds until the giant shadow of Mao Tse Tung loomed across Asia. (When China became a nuclear power the world stopped laughing at the Chinese.)

If the Spanish saved the Filipinos for Christ, the Americans saved them for Coca-Cola and General Motors. While Spain carried its cross on a journey to inspect the potential riches of trade with the East, the American ships and occupation forces were the vanguard of American businessmen looking for new markets in the Orient. That they were joined in their cry to take the islands by a few soul savers who wanted greener fields for their gospel was another historical gaffe. No one apparently among the American Protestant would-be missionaries had been told that the Philippines was the stronghold of Roman Catholicism in Asia, with ninety percent of its then six and a half million population already converted. Religionists and industrialists agreed, however, that it was the obligation of a great and rich nation to guide the less fortunate, and McKinley consoled himself with the idea that taking over the small country would give it protection from being gobbled up by other big, less benign powers, such as Germany.

The benign and godly take-over, however, ended up requiring more military might than had America's war with Spain. The Spanish American War lasted only three months. It took American forces three years to subjugate the Filipinos who were buoyed up and battling from the success of their recent revolt against Spain and furious at the Americans for betraying them.

The United States government and military had assumed that the Philippine blow for independence was confined to a scattering of disorganized insurgents. None seemed aware that the Philippine fight for independence actually was a nationalist movement against colonialism which represented two-thirds of the country's citizens. American reports said the fighting was being waged by "a few Tagalogs" when in fact it was a war enthusiastically joined by all Filipinos except the Muslims in Mindanao.

Because of this unfortunate misrepresentation, the

United States found its efforts to "guide the unfortunate" required the military subjugation of an entire people (and even after Aguinaldo was captured and his official rebel army disbanded, the United States occupation forces found themselves subjected to their first lethal dose of guerrilla warfare from the patriots who kept on sniping at them for another four years).

Nor did the enlightened American forces have any better luck controlling the Muslims in Mindanao than had their Spanish predecessors. When the United States first took control of the Philippines, at the request of the reigning sultan of Sulu, a separate treaty was negotiated with the Muslims in Sulu and a "Moro Province" created which included both Sulu and Mindanao. The United States soon found, however, that this one treaty was insufficient to contain or control all the fiercely independent Muslims. The United States then sought to subjugate the Muslims by arms, and found itself caught up in the costly Moro Wars in which the Muslims were systematically decimated, at a large price in arms and men on both sides, by forces under former Rough Rider General Leonard Wood and General John Pershing. Besides killing off a large segment of the Muslim population (most notably in the shameful massacre of Bud Dajo which has been likened to My Lai), the United States's war against the Muslims further ostracized them from the Christian nation.

In its forty-four years' administration of the Philippines the American government did nothing to heal the unfortunate fracture between the Muslim and Christian Filipinos, nor did it make any attempt to integrate the Muslims into the government. The only time the Muslim and Christian Filipinos presented a united front was during World War II when they joined in their common fight against the Japanese invaders.

From the outset American rule of the Philippines was characterized by a curious and confusing (to the Filipinos) combination of blatant self-interest and high-minded ideals. This dichotomy was evident from the start: while thousands of selfless, dedicated teachers, doctors, and engineers poured in on every boat to set up needed health services and educational facilities and build roads and bridges, at the same time business interests viewed the agricultural Philippines as an exploitable new market for American goods. The theory of "free trade" and free enterprise would mean that Philippine raw materials traveled to the United States and United States products were returned to the Philippines. To keep such a lucrative new market flourishing, Filipinos would be educated to be consumers and industrialization would be kept at a minimum.

Filipinos dutifully developed a passion for American exports: cigarettes, clothing, flour, soft drinks—trading in the ubiquitous calamansi juice of their ancestors for the questionable properties of commercial colas—to such an extent that it was joked that the islands had been "cola-ized" instead of colonized—a fact that apparently was not included in the pretrip briefing given President Nixon, who arrived in Manila with luggage which included cases of Pepsi-Cola. ("He brought his own cola!" Filipinos, whose stores are stocked to the ceiling with soft drinks, murmured incredulously.)

Under the tutelage of American business interests, the Philippines developed a consumer economy of such proportions that they became the largest world market for American wheat flour, cotton textiles, and cigarettes.

With production officially discouraged at home, Filipinos were soon complaining that they were using soap made in New Jersey from Philippine coconut oil—and paying at both ends, in export taxes and taxes on imported products.

The nurturing of tastes for American consumer goods in the Filipinos is in itself questionable. But the biggest charge against the big-business-oriented American-style colonialism lies in the cavalier lack of economic development of the islands which is a legacy that haunts the country to this day. So far as both Spanish and American rule is concerned, Philippine resources were viewed simply as an inexhaustible supply of raw materials which could be hauled home. There was no effort made under either rule to process any of these materials on Philippine soil, or exploit the rich mineral resources of the islands, which might have provided employment that could have substantially spurred the economy and helped develop a middle class. American interests did take advantage of the gold available in the Mountain Province, where the Benguet mines were developed, but nothing was done about the less dramatically rich veins of copper, nickel, etc. A survey in 1970 showed that Philippine mineral resources have been only five percent developed.

On the plus side, the Americans, like the British in India, did train the natives for self-rule. For each post in the American government in the Philippines there was a Filipino understudy to learn the functions of the job. (In contrast to this relatively enlightened approach to governing Asians, the Dutch did nothing of the sort in Indonesia, with the result that when they did pull out there were no natives trained for the task of running a government.)

The Americans, however, did the Philippines a disservice in selecting the obviously best-equipped Filipinos —in terms of education, social graces, etc.—to train for these future government posts, Filipinos who were, in fact, the country's aristocracy, drawn from the wealthy and landowning class. Instead of backing nationalist leaders such as Mabini who might have represented the interests of the masses, the Americans filled the upper echelons of the civil government with Filipino elite, men like Legarda, Pardo de Tavera, Araneta—thus perpetuating the feudal order which had characterized four centuries of Spanish rule.

By their choice of oligarchs the Americans reinforced the stratified social structure of rich and poor, blocking the possible development of a middle class which would have provided a healthy base for a democratic government. It was the very rapidity with which America attempted to democratize the Philippines, as a British analyst observed, that virtually insured that political power pass straight into the hands of the oligarchs. The masses of the poor remained dependent on the wealthy for patronage and had little choice but to give them their allegiance. Since the privileged got into government, they in turn dispensed governmental position and favors to protégés, family, and friends. The beginning of this political corruption was already in evidence by 1920 in the civil service which was discovered, upon investigation, to have the majority of Filipino employees interrelated, and the civil service jobs peddled through political influence rather than awarded on the basis of training or merit.

American paternalism (free public schools, health services, etc.) included no effort at altering or reforming the feudal social structure. The free enterprise theory which dictated the economic scene allowed for an American monopoly on trade and products and the development of American and Filipino economic dynasties, but the trade boom was not felt by the mass of people who, while they now had schools and hygiene, had no more of a piece of the economic or financial pie than they ever had. Spanish serfdom was replaced by "enlightened" tenancy. No longer gouged for tribute to the Church, the Filipino farmers nonetheless found their "rent money" for the land they tilled spiraling year by year into hopelessly unpaid family debts which ensured financial bondage for the ensuing generations, and social unrest.

The American administration apparently saw no rewards in disturbing the old encomienda Spanish land system—which through crown and Church grants had filtered into Filipino hands, transforming external colonial power into domestic colonial power. The handful of Filipino families who by a stroke of fortune had pleased the Spanish king or the Church—or the representative thereof—had become the undisputed hierarchy, a social inequity which American rule did not see fit to disturb.

The greatest American contribution, on the face of it, lay in the field of education. In 1901 a thousand American teachers arrived in the Philippines on board the U. S. transport *Thomas*, and fanned out over the country to train local personnel and establish a network of public schools. Filipinos, starved for education which had been denied them under Spanish rule, flocked to the schools. In 1903 the literacy rate in the islands was only twenty percent. By 1972 it was eighty-three percent—

second only to Japan in Asia. The American influence planted a high motivation for education which obtains among all Filipinos to this day.

However, even the educational thrust was a mixed blessing, since by using English as the only medium of instruction and using American textbooks written from the American viewpoint the educational process served to cripple nationalism in Filipinos, turning them instead into "brown Americans." From being kept barefoot and ignorant under Spanish rule, the Filipinos were now conscientiously created into carbon-copy Americans, with American knowledge and American tastes, which did not necessarily fit Asian reality.

The American school system also implanted the idea of higher education as status. Everyone began to aspire to higher education and professional status with the result that the Philippines has regularly produced many more degreed people than there are jobs for. The lack of employment for highly trained young people has been a serious problem which has resulted in several unfortunate social conditions. First, there is the obvious brain drain as some of the islands' best educated and most able citizens have had to go abroad to find work. Then the numbers of young, college-educated people who are jobless have provided fertile ground for protest and radicalism. It has also lessened the value of a college degree. In the past few years, for instance, degrees in education, commerce, liberal arts, and law have been rendered relatively meaningless in terms of available employment. There are nearly three times as many teachers being graduated from Filipino colleges as the national educational system can absorb.

The second "good" thing the Americans did—which perhaps should rank first, considering its effect on human life—was to introduce sanitation and concepts of public health to the islands, which cut down sharply on the incidence of cholera, typhoid, and smallpox. Public health was taught through the network of schools throughout the rural areas and American-style outhouses began to bloom across the face of the islands. The health instruction also served to educate rural Filipinos against their former dread of hospital care.

Other pluses that can be claimed for the American way of colonialism were a system of transport and communications, and the introduction of the concept of organized labor. Agricultural laborers were unionized during the commonwealth days, although the Americans did nothing to disturb the status quo of inequitable land distribution.

The major crime, in fact, which can be totted up directly against America is its reinforcement of the stratified social structure. The only Filipinos the Americans dealt with were the already entrenched hierarchy of educated landowners. No efforts were made to reach the poorer nationalist leaders or attempt to indoctrinate any but the already wealthy in the intricacies of the democratic process. Rather than attempt to democratize the two-class order, Americans taught the tenets of democracy and free enterprise to the wealthy class.

As it came to know its new rulers, the Philippines soon assembled a cast of American characters—heroes and villains. The first Americans to assess accurately the Filipino character and the nationalist spirit of the country were General Arthur MacArthur (father of Douglas Mac-

A Very Special Relationship   89

Arthur), who arrived with the Third Expeditionary
Force dispatched to the Philippines, and Judge William
Howard Taft, whom McKinley called upon to become
the civil governor of the new colony. It was Arthur Mac-
Arthur who was the first to set the record straight in
Washington, and reported from Manila that the Filipino
revolution was waged by no small band of Tagalogs, as
Commodore Dewey had carelessly reported, but was in
actual fact a national revolution, and that the Filipinos
were united in their revolution against Spain.

As military governor, he subjugated the islands by military force, and then held them under martial law. But he
issued a lenient proclamation of amnesty that promised a
reward and no punishment for turning over firearms. And
he religiously punished all American officers found guilty
of mistreating Filipinos.

Tough, but fair, MacArthur won the respect and trust
of Filipinos—so much so that a number of patriots who
kept up guerrilla activities against the United States military over a period of several years when they finally did
surrender did so on condition that they would surrender
"only to MacArthur."

While the country was still under martial law, General
MacArthur also proclaimed the writ of habeas corpus—
an innovative and daring thing to do in a country that
was still in armed conflict. And, unlike many of the racist
members of the military hierarchy, MacArthur personally
attempted to befriend the Filipinos. He organized a Filipino branch of the military, called the Scouts, to serve
under American officers. These men, many of whom had
fought against Spain, and subsequently against the American forces, took the oath of allegiance to the United

States and were later to become the nucleus of the American armed forces in the Philippines.

Unfortunately, since they shared a democratic and realistic view of the country, MacArthur and Taft clashed personally, over military versus civilian control—a fight so bitter there was not enough room in the little country for the two of them. In the inevitable showdown, Taft won and MacArthur was recalled to the United States. But MacArthur's feeling for and understanding of the islands was to be reflected later in the emergence of his son as the greatest non-Filipino champion the islands would ever know.

Judge Taft, as McKinley and that other isolationist Ohioan Secretary of State Judge Day, didn't like anything about this new American imperialism. When President McKinley first fingered him for the job of civil governor of the islands, Taft said, "Mr. President, I'm sorry we have got the Philippines. I don't want them and I think you ought to have some man who is more in sympathy with the situation." To which the President had answered, "You don't want them any less than I do. But we have got them and in dealing with them I think I can trust the man who didn't want them better than I can the man who did."

McKinley himself emerges in the Philippine view as neither villain nor hero—an insular American uninformed about Asia, who basically meant well and did not feel comfortable with the idea of gobbling up smaller countries.

The Philippine American presidential heroes are Woodrow Wilson, Franklin Roosevelt, and Harry Truman. Wilson because he signed the Jones Act in 1916, which was the first official acknowledgment of the islands' desire for independence and gave the Filipinos an elective Senate to replace the American dominated Philippine Commission; Roosevelt because he signed the Tydings-McDuffie Act in 1934, which established a commonwealth government for the Philippines with the official promise of complete independence in ten years (after Hoover had vetoed it); and Truman, who signed the final Independence Act.

These triumphs for Philippine nationalism were not bestowed out of sheer generosity. They had been fought for every inch of the way since the ban was first lifted on nationalist parties in 1906 and Filipino nationalists could come out of hiding and openly wage their battle for independence. (Prior to 1906 the only party allowed was the Federal party which espoused annexation of the Philippines to the United States.) In 1906, as soon as the ban was lifted, a nationalist party sprang full bloom into view, headed by two equally ardent patriots, the handsome, fiery, and charismatic mestizo Manuel L. Quezon, a man of humble origin, educated by the friars, who had been a major in Aguinaldo's army; and the scholarly, mild-mannered Sergio Osmeña, of Chinese extraction, who belonged to the country's minuscule middle class. When a National Assembly was created in 1907, Osmeña was elected speaker and Quezon was elected floor leader of the majority and sent as Resident Commissioner of the Philippines to Washington. (The moment nationalism was allowed the pro-American Federalist party died an unremarked death.) The fight for Philippine independence was then waged vigorously on two fronts by Osmeña in Manila and Quezon in Washington.

President Wilson's handpicked appointee, Governor General Francis Burton Harrison, was another Philippine hero (and a horror to the United States imperialists in Manila and at home). A committed libertarian, Harrison, with his President's approval, pursued a policy of "Filipinization," even giving the Filipinos their first judicial powers. (According to the Republican press, the country promptly went to hell.)

But with the change of administration in Washington from Wilson to Harding, in 1921, the official American position alternated from helpful to harsh. In the familiar United States political pattern where a liberal president is followed by a reactionary one whose first act is to back off or attempt to kill any reforms his predecessor may have made, Harding (big business's favorite son) promptly backed off the Wilsonian policy of independence for the Philippines, and put in a hard-nosed administrator to "straighten out the mess" over there and establish "law and order." Harding's "man in Manila," General Leonard Wood, tried to reverse all the "Filipinization" policies set in motion by Harrison.

Where Harrison had succeeded in winning the respect and cooperation of Filipinos, Wood antagonized them from the outset—so violently that the entire Filipino cabinet resigned. Wood reacted to that by abolishing the Council of State, and he administered the country through his own military coterie, with little respect for Filipino opinion.

The sugar industry in the Philippines, its major export, was originally controlled by British, Spanish, Dutch, and Americans. As soon as the Filipinos had the legislative power to do so, under the leadership of Quezon a

Philippines National Bank was organized in order that Filipinos would have a chance to buy into their own major industry. This move was violently opposed by General Wood who claimed that the Philippine National Bank was opened only so that Filipino politicians could get their hands on the national till, a viewpoint which was given much publicity in the pro-Harding press. To show his absolute opposition to such a move, General Wood jailed the first president of the Philippine bank. Without a national bank, however, which Quezon did succeed in establishing, the country's major industry would still be in the control of foreigners. It was Quezon's view that indigenous sugar barons were a lesser evil than foreign ones. ("I would rather have a government run like hell by Filipinos than like heaven by Americans," he once voiced the battle cry of the nationalists.)

Wood apparently could not understand Filipino pride or nationalism. Convinced that the Filipinos were "better off" under benevolent American rule and should appreciate it, he felt personally betrayed when the Filipinos were not grateful—in much the same way the patriarchal southerner felt when he discovered that his blacks didn't really like being slaves. When Carlos P. Romulo, a Quezon man who was a newspaper editor before becoming President Quezon's personal secretary, wrote an editorial attacking Wood's anti-Philippine administration, Wood was angered, embittered, and felt betrayed, as he told Romulo, that any young man who had enjoyed the advantages of an American university would be so ungrateful as to attack America.

It was a viewpoint which was to haunt Philippine-American relations through the years. Express a "Filipino point of view or a nationalist desire," and you were "biting the hand that feeds you" and betraying your benefactor.

General Wood was actually an able administrator—he could balance a budget with the best of them—but he did not understand the Filipino desire for self-government. Also, as a member of the military establishment, Wood was inherently racist in regard to Asians and viewed them as inferior intellectually and socially, as incapable of the demands of government as of society. The proud, brilliant, and elegant Quezon fought Wood inch by inch —in a running duel that was to exhaust them both. It is thought that their constant sparring actually was a contributing factor both to Wood's early death (of a brain tumor while still in office in 1927) and Quezon's losing fight with tuberculosis.

Henry L. Stimson, who followed Wood, can be numbered among the "good guys" from the Philippine viewpoint, since he showed respect and encouragement for Philippine development, and set a social precedent by the inclusion of at least fifty percent Filipinos in the official parties given by the Governor General at Malacanang Palace. Stimson also reintroduced the Philippine ceremonial dance, the *rigodon de honor*, at these parties—a pretty gesture which endeared him to Manila society.

In 1935 the Philippines, which had been a territorial possession, became, through the implementation of the Tydings-McDuffie Act, a commonwealth with a government of its own and executive powers. The Supreme Court, which had been inching toward full Filipino representation since Governor General Harrison put the first Filipino justices into it, also became entirely Filipino, giving the "native government" judicial rights as well.

The day that the Philippines became a commonwealth and was entitled to fly its own flag at long last, beside that of the United States, the crowds who had gathered wept openly. They had had a few days of independence between their defeat of the Spanish and the attack by the United States forces nearly forty years before—and now once more they were on the road to independence. Manuel Quezon was elected the first president and Sergio Osmeña became vice-president. The last U.S. Governor General, Frank Murphy, became the first U.S. High Commissioner, and turned the Philippine White House, Malacanang Palace, over to the Filipino president.

Quezon and Osmeña had received aid in their fight for Philippine independence from American labor unions, who wanted to stop Philippine immigration, and from farm lobbies who wanted to put a halt to dutyfree imports. The original bill for Philippine independence that was brought before Congress was turned down by the prescient Quezon, however, because it granted the United States the right to develop military and naval bases in the Philippines. He worked for and got, instead, a compromise bill, in the Tydings-McDuffie Act, which left the matter of bases in the Philippines to future arrangement.

Before the commonwealth period, the prevailing attitude of the American press was to show that the Philippines was incapable of self-rule. Writers such as Kenneth Roberts and Katherine Mayo justified American imperialism in articles that appeared regularly in *Colliers* and *The Saturday Evening Post* designed to show that the Filipinos were little more than uncivilized barbarians warring with one another. Newspapers carried "authoritative" accounts of the Philippines which, they said, was made up of so many warring tribes that they would be at each other's throats if allowed to run their own country. (The Ilocanos would be against the Pampangos who would be fighting the Tagalogs, etc.)

In Mayo's book-length denigration of the Philippines (*Isles of Fear*, 1924), her racist arguments are only too hauntingly reminiscent of southern white supremacists' justifications for slavery: she refers to Filipinos as "wild men," "primitive peons," and states categorically that the Malay's inferiority to the Anglo-Saxon is "simply a biological fact." According to her version, the Americans, happening upon the islands, discovered conditions that "outraged every tenet of Yankee decency." "Ablaze with pity [she didn't happen to mention the death of the natives at American hands in either the three years of fighting the revolutionists or the massacre of the Muslims in the Moro Wars] and with righteous wrath, our people flew at the islands like a White-Wing brigade in a sort of Holy War upon ignorance, superstition, disease, and dirt. . . . "

The "villains" in Miss Mayo's league were the men like Woodrow Wilson or Governor Harrison, who thought the Filipinos had a right to rule themselves. She put forth the theory that the Great White Father was the only thing standing between exploitation of the natives by the landowners (who were, in fact, precisely those Filipinos whom the United States administration, from Taft on, had always backed). She also stated categorically that following the Jones Act, when the Philippines was given some autonomy, it was nothing but a downhill course of "destruction, decay, and loot."

Some of the distorted press could be traced to the

pragmatic, straight-talking Americans' misunderstanding
of Asian ritual politeness and face-saving. American newsmen who came to the Philippines and were entertained
by Filipinos would ask confidentially, "What do you think
about independence?," and the Filipino host, knowing
precisely what the American wanted to hear and not
wanting to hurt his feelings by unpleasant truths, would
hedge, murmuring politely, "Well, we like the Americans.
. . ." Then the journalist would dash home and write a
feature story on how the Filipinos really wanted the
United States to continue to control their country.

Part of the American attitude also could be traced to
the racism (acknowledged or not) of the white-skinned
person in Asia. "The colonel's lady" in Manila could live
like a queen on her American dollar which provided her
with four little brown women to do all her chores—for the
cost of a once-a-week cleaning woman back home. She
had maids, nursemaids, seamstresses. And her attitude
toward the natives who provided the cheap labor was
inevitable superiority. Lorraine Carr, an American army
wife, recalled, in her book *To the Philippines with Love,*
that when she arrived in the Philippines in 1945 she was
advised by the American colony, "Don't deal socially with
Filipinos." They, she was told, were for servants, but not
equals.

The American colony excluded "natives" from such
private clubs as the Manila Polo Club, the Manila Army
and Navy Club, and the Baguio Country Club in the
lovely mountain retreat where the government's summer
capital is located. When this was brought to the attention
of Quezon at the time he was president of the Senate, he
sent word to the Filipino owners of the club land at

Baguio that they should notify the club that its lease would be canceled if it did not admit Filipinos. The club owners backed down at the threat of losing their beautiful site, and Filipinos have been using the club ever since. The situation at the Manila Polo Club, which was patronized by American army officers, American civilians, and Spanish Filipinos was handled in a more complicated fashion. "Liberal" members of the club, the Spanish Elizalde brothers, who were Filipino citizens but club members because they had no Malay blood, were approached and a test case set up in which a Filipino aide to Quezon attempted entrance and was blackballed, wherewith the liberals resigned and built their own club.

As soon as he had the executive power to do so, President Quezon showed his awareness of the Philippines' basic social ills by launching a program of public works and purchase of land for settlement. Laws which granted more rights to the working class and legal assistance for the poor were enacted. Efforts were made to promote Filipino ownership and development of agriculture and small industry. Muslim Sulu was wooed into the commonwealth, and the former sultanate abolished. In the interests of national defense, Quezon engineered the passage of a law providing for the organization of a Philippine armed force, and called upon his old friend, former U.S. Chief of Staff General Douglas MacArthur, whom Quezon had known both in the Philippines and in Washington, to serve as military advisor to the commonwealth government—a job which carried with it the rank of field marshal in the Philippine army.

Once the Filipinos had the reins of government in their own hands, the United States posture was to downgrade everything they did. Sources of so-called black propaganda about the government could invariably be traced to the high commissioner's office, and later, after independence, to the embassy that displayed the cavalier contempt of a former lover. ("Believe me, I know her—and she's no good.") On a visit to India after that country had received its independence, a Filipino editor was surprised to find, in contrast, the resident British speaking only well of the Indian government. When he asked why, his British friends replied, "We'd be poor teachers, wouldn't we, if we thought our students couldn't run a government!" America, however, tended to downgrade its former colony, forgetting they had indeed been its tutors. In an appalling putdown of the tragic drama enacted during the fall of the Philippines at the outset of World War II, the American press referred to the 100,000 Filipino soldiers who fought and died along with the American forces as "MacArthur's Boy Scouts."

When the Japanese attacked Manila in 1941, Quezon and his vice-president, Osmeña, joined General MacArthur, who had been recalled to active duty with the United States to command Philippine military forces, on the Rock, at Corregidor. Then President Roosevelt arranged to have the ailing Philippine president rescued by submarine and flown to the United States.

MacArthur had promised his friend, "I'll put you back in Malacanang Palace, Mr. President, if I must put you back on the points of our bayonets."

But Quezon was to die of tuberculosis at Saranac Lake, New York, before the Allies retook Manila. Upon Quezon's death Osmeña, who was also by then in exile in the United States, became president. He and MacArthur's

aide Romulo were, at MacArthur's invitation, with the
General when the Allied troops landed at Leyte, and the
task of freeing the Philippines began once more.

But what they found, following the four years of Japanese occupation, was enough to make the country's upcoming independence academic.

5

The Ruined City

When General Eisenhower saw the ruins of Manila in 1944, after MacArthur's forces had retaken the city from the Japanese, he commented that "only Warsaw" had suffered such utter devastation. A British observer likened the once gay and beautiful port to a crematorium.

Eighty percent of the city was destroyed. It lay, black and reeking, smashed from above by American bombers, gutted below in the fanatic last stand made by a renegade detachment of Japanese marines who had disobeyed the evacuation orders of the high command and elected to die with the city. Realizing they were trapped, they had holed in at the walled inner city, Intramuros, then systematically destroyed much of Manila and its citizens as the liberation forces moved nearer. In the final weeks and days before the city was retaken, houses were burned or sacked, the last food supplies destroyed. Thousands of civilians were rendered homeless, starving, living in caves and dugouts. All the dogs and cats had been killed for food. Corpses were buried naked in shallow graves, their rags stolen to be sold for food. With health services completely broken down, many who had escaped death by gun or bayonet fell victim to disease. Roving gangs of half-clothed youngsters scavenged and stole.

In the sick last-ditch purge, entire families who had survived the occupation were massacred. A Filipino officer with MacArthur hurried to his home—to find the freshly bayoneted bodies of his father, mother, two sisters, and a brother strewn like broken dolls across the garden of the house.

Another officer went to his family home to be greeted with a grotesque tableau: the bodies of his brother and sister-in-law lying across their car where they had been ambushed, and the body of his father sprawled on the front steps, where he apparently had died from a heart attack as he witnessed their murder.

Still a third located the site of his house to find nothing but smoldering ashes. The Japanese soldiers who had used it set fire to it as they left. Next door, across the fence they had once shared, the officer found the body of his neighbor, a mining engineer, lying face down in the front yard. In his diary, he recorded, "Saw our house . . . nothing but ashes and ruins . . . have not found my wife or my sons. I am broken hearted. . . ." The wife and a son of Senator Elpidio Quirino, who was later to become president of the Philippines, were also shot and killed by the Japanese as they retreated from Manila.

When he made his way to the family compound of friends with whom he had left his personal effects during the war, Commander Chick Parsons found that everyone there—family and servants—had just been murdered. "There were 25 bodies." he recalls. "People forget that the civilians here went through two wars—when the Philippines was taken, and then, again, when it was liberated."

Parsons' American mother-in-law had been beheaded early in the occupation when she refused to disclose his whereabouts. General Romulo's mother had been beaten and crippled for a similar refusal to give information about her son.

The savagery directed against the Filipinos by the Japanese was in retaliation for the Filipinos' unswerving loyalty to America. Throughout their helpless, hopeless three years of occupation, the Filipino people had never yielded to the Japanese. Organized guerrilla resistance had begun within six months after the fall of Bataan and Corregidor.

After General MacArthur was ordered off Corregidor by President Roosevelt, the remaining American and Filipino troops, under the command of General Jonathan M. Wainwright, had waged a defensive action that stands today as a marvel of bravery and fortitude. Without adequate food, medical supplies, or ammunition and no hope of getting any they had hung on nonetheless for five months before Bataan finally fell, Corregidor was overrun, and General Wainwright was taken prisoner.

Some of those troops, however, refused to obey Wainwright's surrender order and hid out instead in the jungle and mountain fastnesses of Luzon where they furnished the nucleus of what was to become a massive Philippine resistance group. Not only tacitly supported, but actively aided and protected by the majority of Filipinos, despite savage retaliation by the Japanese occupation forces, the guerrillas carried out widespread effective sabotage operations against the Japanese throughout the occupation, and paved the way for MacArthur's eventual reentry into the Philippines.

The guerrillas were in constant touch by radio with General MacArthur, in Australia. At the time the Japanese took Manila, three civilian Filipinos, who had been employees of a radio station in Manila, escaped by rowboat from Luzon with a load of radio supplies and established a shortwave station in a mountain hideout on the island of Panay. When the War Department picked up their signals and alerted MacArthur in Australia, the General sent the Filipino war ace, Colonel Jesus Villamor, by submarine to the Philippines to contact the radio men. Villamor reached the mountain station, and then began to set up an organized resistance radiating out from it. MacArthur next sent an American-born Manila businessman, Commander Charles "Chick" Parsons, to Luzon to comb the island and make contact with the patriots and coordinate the resistance movement into a secret army. President Quezon dispatched one of his personal physicians, Major Egmidio Cruz, to the Philippines to aid in this work, and Cruz was able to reach Manila, where he rendezvoused with the guerrilla leaders. Eventually Villamor, Parsons, and Cruz worked out a communication network that was so successful that the Filipino guerrillas were able to keep MacArthur in hourly touch with the Philippines throughout the Japanese occupation. Radio equipment, food, firearms, and men trained in sabotage and intelligence work were smuggled in to work with them. And when MacArthur was finally ready to move the liberation forces into the Philippines, it was the guerrillas who cleared the civilians out of the way, then prepared for and met the landings of the liberation forces on Mindanao, Leyte, and Luzon.

Little known except to those who participated in it, the Philippine resistance did not, like the French *maquis*, have its novelists and movie-script writers to give it world-wide publicity after the war. But in many ways it faced dangers even more devastating than did the *maquis*. For the Filipinos there were no convenient European borders to slip across, as the French resistance fighters had in Switzerland and Spain. And the Gestapo, vicious as it was, was no match for the efficient Oriental terrorism practiced by the Japanese. Rather than the mass murder carried out by the Nazis, the Japanese practiced the cen-turies-old Oriental savagery against the individual that is designed to terrorize and demoralize the observers. As the American general Charles Willoughby, who compiled a record of the Philippine resistance, observed, the firing squad cannot compare in brutality to an Oriental behead-ing—especially when the executioner is an amateur.

There was a macabre wartime joke in the Philippines that the one good thing you could say for the occupation was that, for one time in the country's history, all its citizens were in the same boat: equal victims. Former or future power or wealth gave a man no edge over his neighbor in survival under the Japanese. Each individual ran the same chance of being brutally murdered.

Ironically, considering the devastation they wreaked on the islands and the inhabitants, the Japanese actually had nothing against the Filipinos at the beginning of the war. They would never have attacked the Philippines were it not for the presence of American bases and American military forces. As fellow Asians, the Japanese assumed that when they took the Philippines they could win the cooperation of the Filipinos against the white man—as had proved true in the other countries of south-east Asia which had surrendered to or cooperated with Japan: Burma, Indonesia, Thailand. But curiously, the

Filipinos opted for loyalty to America—the only former western colony in Asia to do so. Perhaps because of the excesses of imperialism, most notably the social practice of racial superiority, the English, Dutch, and French colonies all sided with Japan.

Only the Filipinos held firm and remained loyal to America. And it was a loyalty which was to cost them dearly in terms of the destruction to their country and loss of civilian life. For, within months after occupying the islands, when the Japanese realized that the Filipinos remained their intractable foes and refused outright to join in the "greater East Asia Co-Prosperity Sphere," the "Asia for Asians" plan offered them by the Japanese, the Japanese were furious and turned their fury on the Filipino civilian population. Entire villages were destroyed by the occupation forces, down to the last child and chicken. Individual torture killings were frequent. Rape/murders and beheadings were the order of the day.

It was in this terrifying atmosphere that the Filipino guerrillas functioned, carrying out an elaborate network of resistance and communication which helped MacArthur to make good his promise to return. And in their years of operation, no guerrilla, Filipino or American, was known to have been betrayed by a civilian. That the guerrillas were so universally protected by the civilians throughout the islands further enraged the occupation forces and provoked ghoulish criminal acts. Yet the Filipinos endured murder, rape, and torture without betraying the silent forces in their midst. During these years five percent of the total population was destroyed. Many of the remainder suffered mutilations and tortures that marked them for life. Yet there is no evidence of any betrayals. As an example of how "tight" civilian security was, when a Filipino officer's eldest son was commissioned by General MacArthur to locate his own mother and younger brothers and rescue them, the people of three villages who knew where the family was hiding refused to tell him where they were until he finally, in desperation, was able to locate a group of guerrillas the villagers knew who would come and vouch for his identity.

There was one moment, early in the war, when the Philippines's president, Manuel Quezon, foreseeing the inevitable deprivation, destruction, and loss of life during the occupation, considered surrendering to the Japanese.

On Corregidor, after it had become apparent that American aid was not forthcoming, Quezon decided, in order to avert the total destruction of his country and needless suffering of its people, he should go back into Manila, ask the Filipino forces to stop fighting and surrender, and request Japan to neutralize the islands, thus saving them from the ravages of war.

It was clear that America had abandoned the Philippines, at least temporarily. At the first burst of gunfire, the American navy that had been in Manila Bay was ordered out to Java. American and Filipino ground forces had no naval or air support and no incoming supplies of food or ammunition, nor any hope of any. Despite his close friendship with MacArthur, it looked to President Quezon like a useless sacrifice. He called a meeting of the Filipino leaders who were with him on Corregidor: Vice-President Osmeña, Roxas, and the Chief Justice, Abad Santos. Although Osmeña, Roxas, and Abad Santos all vigorously opposed Quezon's plan, a cable was drafted by the Chief Justice at Quezon's behest to President Roosevelt, stating Quezon's plan for surrender. It was given to General MacArthur, who sent it without comment.

Roosevelt returned a spirited reply, which said, in effect, to Quezon that "if this is your decision, Mr. President, go ahead. However, I will instruct the American forces to continue to fight to the last in the defense of the Philippines. . . ."

Quezon could not surrender in the face of such fighting words. He changed his mind. Roosevelt eventually made arrangements for the Philippine President and his family and Vice-President Osmeña to be rescued from Corregidor and taken to the United States where a Philippine government in exile was established. When Quezon died, in 1944, before the liberation of the Philippines, his vice-president, Sergio Osmeña, was sworn in as president in exile. Osmeña appointed MacArthur's aide General Romulo to be resident commissioner of the Philippines to the United States, and as such he was a member of the American Congress. Then the two of them rejoined MacArthur for the D-Day landing on Leyte.

As soon as the liberation forces set foot on Philippine soil MacArthur turned the reins of civil government over to President Osmeña, who proceeded to get a civil government into action weeks before Manila was retaken and months before the islands were entirely freed.

As they retreated the Japanese systematically stripped the country of all its crops, fowl, and animals, carrying with them everything that could be used, burning and destroying the rest. The cattle industry, for example, has never recovered, since all the breeding stock on the islands was either decimated or used for food by the Japanese army at that time. Vegetables and fruits were stripped, then the vines and trees destroyed. Press correspondents reported that as MacArthur's forces swept across the islands toward Manila they kept seeing queer-looking little old wizened Filipinos—and then realized to their horror that these were the country's children.

The islands' economy was shattered, the civilian population destitute and diseased. Manila lay in ashes. It was upon these ashes that the Philippines was to build its new republic.

Soon after the liberation, when the first election was held, General Manuel Roxas succeeded the quiet, scholarly Osmeña as president. (Concerned with the insurmountable tasks of his office, Osmeña didn't bother to leave the palace to campaign, with the result that the charismatic and eloquent Roxas swept the imagination and the votes of a sick, impoverished, and demoralized population.)

A close associate of MacArthur, Roxas had served with him on Bataan and Corregidor, and, before the fall of Bataan, had escaped and made his way to Mindanao where he was finally captured by the Japanese and taken to Manila.

Repeatedly approached by the Japanese to participate in the government, Roxas feigned illness for over two years and then, at last, when his excuse had worn dangerously thin, he accepted a minor advisory position with the puppet government. Because of this, he suffered in American eyes, or at least in the eyes of the American Secretary of the Interior, Harold Ickes, under whom Philippine affairs was administered, from the taint of collaboration.

Considering the high price so many Filipinos had paid for their patriotism, the outside world found the islands' apparent leniency toward its collaborators difficult to understand. Why, demanded the fire-eating Ickes, was not a man like Laurel (who had served as president of the occupation government) tried and executed? Why didn't the Filipinos kill off their known collaborators, such as Laurel, Recto, Aquino, or Vargas, as the Italians and French had done? Shave their heads. Execute them by firing squad. A United States commission, sent to investigate Philippine collaboration, turned in a report which recommended harsh treatment—the news of which had greeted MacArthur on his landing in Leyte. Secretary Ickes wanted to come to Manila and see for himself— a contretemps which MacArthur, who understood the temper of the Philippines, ardently wished to avoid.

There had been ambivalence about the collaborators among Filipinos at first. When the Japanese first took Manila, the "Voice of Freedom" from Corregidor broadcast a blistering attack on the men who had helped the Japanese General Homma set up an occupation government: Laurel, Recto, and Vargas. After the broadcast, President Quezon sent for the commentator and gave him hell.

"It's not true those men are traitors," Quezon told him. He explained that one of the last things he had done, as president, before leaving Manila, was to call in his cabinet and the political leaders and tell them: "The thing you must keep uppermost in mind is to protect the civilian population as best you can." If the Philippines' own political leaders did not take the government jobs, Quezon pointed out, those top positions would go to such men as Artemio Ricarte (alias Vibora), a Filipino revolutionary general who had sought political asylum in Japan rather than give allegiance to America and had accompanied the Japanese to the Philippines. Or they would use Benigno Ramos, a radical newsman, chief of the Sakdals, who had staged an uprising among the peasants of Luzon against Quezon's government. These choices could prove tragic for the civilian population.

Quezon was convinced that the Filipinos who had accepted positions with the government were patriots. "I have faith in them," he told MacArthur. "I'm certain they joined the government in order to carry out my wishes."

Quezon's faith in the collaborators never wavered, and eventually MacArthur, who had at first considered them traitors, came around to Quezon's viewpoint. There was no evidence that the civilians suffered at the hands of their own leaders.

MacArthur held several meetings with President Osmeña at the headquarters of the civil government at Tacloban, before the march on Manila, to discuss, among other pressing matters, the prickly problem of what should be done with the collaborators.

President Osmeña wanted them put under his personal parole, so that he would be solely responsible for them. MacArthur might have favored such a move but, aware of Secretary Ickes's cry for blood, he decided that he could not permit such a lenient disposition of the collaborators without running the risk of offending Washington. So, to appease Ickes, MacArthur chose a middle course, and rounded up the collaborators and interned them in a penal colony on the island of Palawan where they were held for a few months and then released. Considering Ickes's attitude, it was the best MacArthur could do for them, or for President Osmeña. It did succeed in keeping Ickes out of Manila.

But it was a move misunderstood by the collaborators, who held it against both MacArthur and President Osmeña. They took out their resentment against the President by throwing all their political weight and that of their supporters against him at the next election, which contributed to Osmeña's loss to General Roxas.

At the time that MacArthur arrested the collaborators and had them interned, he let Roxas go free. This was because MacArthur was personally convinced that Roxas had remained loyal to his government and America despite the fact that he had taken a position in the occupation government. The intelligence reports which came to MacArthur from the guerrillas had shown that Roxas had actually aided the guerrillas at the time he was serving in the Japanese government.

Although the collaborators were released and never punished, there were mixed feelings about them, and, in the postwar years, in order to justify their position, the men who had collaborated with the Japanese became virulently anti-American and nationalistic. Some of them, for example, who had collaborated with the Japanese, ran on a political platform which demanded that Clark Air Force Base should be dismantled and all American-owned property confiscated and nationalized by the government.

Unfortunately, the actions of the United States toward its former colony in the immediate postwar years played into the hands of the nationalists: in the shabby treatment of Filipino veterans, in the demands for American parity from a prostrate people, in the refusal to finance the kind of postwar aid needed to rebuild a ravished country (while on the other hand giving monumental amounts of aid to Japan).

Brilliant orators and polemicists, the nationalists, especially Laurel and Recto, strongly influenced a generation of war babies—the voters of today—who cut their teeth on their anti-American speeches and tracts. Much of the political opposition to the present government stems from the men who were raised on the oratory and writings of that period.

The nationalists' argument went something like this: The United States had simply pulled out of the Philippines and abandoned it to the Japanese, and left its colony to survive as best it could for three years without any aid. (United States military power was concentrated on the European front.) The treaties between the Philippines and the United States were one-sided, onerous, and unfair. The United States took advantage of the sad plight of the devastated Philippines, at the time it most needed help from America for rehabilitation, to extract special privileges, economically and militarily. When the country was flat on its back the United States exploited its need by exacting special rights that allowed Americans to exploit the country's resources. After Filipinos had bled and died for America, America refused to recognize the rights of its veterans as equal to those of American soldiers.

Unfortunately, much of this was true. That the Filipinos did feel let down and disappointed in the way American treated them after the war was shown by the fact that the country gave its majority support to the anti-American nationalist factions: Laurel and Recto, who were elected by overwhelming majorities to Congress.

In the immediate postwar years the Philippines found that its sentimental attachment to its former colonizer was scarcely reciprocated. American response to Filipino need was dictated by profit-motive pragmatism rather than any sentiment inspired by shared wartime calamity.

In the months immediately prior to Philippine independence Filipino representatives in Washington waged a last-ditch fight to get aid and appropriations which could help the devastated country get back on its feet. Between the ravages of war and the three years of an unusually cruel occupation, agriculture and industry had been virtually destroyed. The economy was wrecked. The people were weak and sick.

Filipinos had been proclaimed "heroes" during the dark days of Bataan and Corregidor, and again at the time of the liberation when it became known that the brave guerrilla forces had cut short the retaking of the islands by many months, thus bringing to a swifter conclusion the war in the Pacific. But by 1946 America had forgotten. The eyes of the embryo world power were focused elsewhere. Germany must be rebuilt. And Japan. The thrust of American foreign policy in Asia was toward preventing the spread of Communism in the Far East, and to prop up the countries most likely to succumb to Communism.

In the American view, the Philippines did not seem threatened. It was a democracy, trained by America itself. It had contained its internal Communism through its own efforts in the past. It could certainly do so again. America concentrated, instead, on Japan and India. If India fell to the Communists, so the American reasoning went, it would mean the failure of democracy in Asia. No one was worried about the loyal little Philippines. They were already imbued with democratic ideals.

The only American eyes on the Philippines in 1946 were those of United States business interests, who saw the decimated little country as ripe for exploitation in mining, import, and export. A combined business lobby was forged, which maintained a series of adjoining rooms in the Mayflower Hotel in Washington, to fight all efforts at Philippine economic independence. Through the efforts of this power bloc the war-ravaged country was forced to grant important concessions to the United States in exchange for economic survival. The United States forced the Philippines actually to rewrite their constitution in order to provide parity for Americans in their country (a humiliation not imposed on Japan, since that country, while defeated, was nonetheless a sovereign nation and not subject to such treatment). In the fight for parity, the lobbyists were given the full support and backing of Paul V. McNutt, former U.S. high commissioner to the Philippines, who had been named as the first American ambassador to the new republic. While commissioner, McNutt had steadfastly opposed Philippine independence, and he threw all his support to the defense of American business interests, against the infant republic. When, after futile opposition to the bill, the Philippines' resident commissioner to the United States, Carlos Romulo, was forced to accept the onerous provisions of the Philippines Trade Act, since it was that or nothing, he said from the floor of Congress:

"This bill, Mr. Speaker, is not the kind I would have written in the best of all possible worlds. In such a world the Philippines would be standing firmly on its own feet, depending on its own resources . . . freed of feudalism and archaic economic politics, independent in its economy as well as in its politics. . . .

". . . if I had written this bill as I would have wished, it would provide for perpetual free trade between the United States and the Philippines, amid a global community of perpetual free trade. It would provide for no graduated tariffs, no quotas, no limitations on commerce.

"If I had written it, the rights assured to the United

States would not appear in the bill at all. They would be assured by a treaty entered into on a basis of complete equality between our two sovereign nations. . . ."

Yet at the same time, while forcing economic privileges from the Philippines, the United States Congress refused to give Filipino veterans equal benefits with American soldiers. Unlike any other foreign soldiers who had served in the American forces, the only rights the Filipino veterans were allowed to share equally with American veterans were funeral rights. Otherwise their allotment was one peso to the American dollar—less than one half as much. The Communists in the Philippines had a field day with the veterans' tangible disappointment at this inequity.

On its knees, the Philippines was forced to make deals at whatever cost, since complete economic independence at this stage would have meant total bankruptcy. The country's exports, from liberation in October 1944 until the Trade Bill was passed in 1945, amounted to less than one million dollars. The Philippines' prewar exports had averaged $155 million annually.

The only thing the country had to sell in any quantity, that had not been ruined by the war, was sugar. The Philippines had to have a monopoly on the United States market for its major product. But in exchange for the preferential trade rates which it needed, the country was forced to give up land for military bases, and rewrite its constitution to provide a parity rights amendment which gave Americans equal rights to the resources of the country.

This parity agreement was to fuel anti-American feelings for years to come. A unilateral arrangement, in the name of free trade, it was the price the Philippines paid for stability and friendship with the United States. "There is no free trade or free and open competition between a giant and a pigmy," as one Filipino commented bitterly, "or a lion and a mouse." In order to get the preferential trade agreement they had to have to survive, the Philippines was forced by America to accept its military and economic will.

In a blatant erosion of the sovereignty of another country, the United States demanded—and got—from the helpless Philippines a ninety-nine-year lease on Clark Air Force Base, the only time in the world that one country has granted another country a ninety-nine-year lease. For the price of the sugar quota the United States also imposed on the Philippines the stricture that its former colony could not purchase any munitions from any other country, and could only buy munitions in the amount approved by the United States. These were hardly the terms of a long-promised independence and sovereignty.

President Quezon had warned against—and waged a successful fight against—the establishment of American bases on free Philippine soil. He had refused to approve the Philippines Independence Act until that clause was deleted. But now the presence of American bases could no longer be avoided. The Philippines no longer had any bargaining position. A destroyed, impoverished country, it had to get aid somewhere. And there was nowhere else to turn. No other major power was interested in financing the Philippines, or offering them a hand after the war. Britain, France, Holland all had their own fish to fry— their own ex-colonies who needed their aid.

Through UNRRA (the United Nations Rehabilitation and Reconstruction Agency) the Philippines was finally allotted a total of $12 million for national rehabilitation.

The fact sheet on which this allotment was based showed that the little country had suffered wartime losses of 89,000 people and $860,872,000 in property damage.

The Philippines received its long-awaited independence on July 4, 1946. General Roxas became the first president of the Philippine Republic. To ensure that the government's offices and documents would not be subject to destruction by bombs in future wars, the site of the capital was moved from Manila proper (which as a harbor is subject to attack) to nearby Quezon City where the University of the Philippines is located.

The Philippines was free—but not free. The country had achieved political independence. But economically it was as dependent upon the United States as it had been in its commonwealth days. The American concept of government for the country and its economic development (as envisaged and controlled by American business interests) had worked at cross purposes. While the country was promised, and trained for, self-government on the political front, it was kept in economic bondage by a hothouse economy in which the islands depended on United States preferential trade agreements to absorb its raw materials, in exchange gobbling up United States-made consumer goods, without any move to produce them.

When the United States gave the Philippines its independence, it was a political independence only, for it maintained much of its colonial economic and military advantages. Independent in name, the Philippines's economic and industrial growth was still at the mercy of alien interests.

There was talk in the Philippines that President Roxas should have done better by his country. (When he made a speech in favor of the parity amendment, he narrowly escaped death when bombs were exploded on the speaker's platform.) It was thought—especially by the nationalists—that he should have held out for more benefits, more aid. But, because of the American suspicion of collaboration, Roxas had found himself in an extremely delicate and awkward position in his dealings with the United States. In order to prove his loyalty, he had given in to almost all of the excessive demands made by America in regard to military bases and funding for rehabilitation.

The enemy of Philippine freedom and development was not the American Congress, but American business interests who had the ear, arm, or pocket of Congress. Few politicians would risk losing their political office in order to support the Philippines's position, no matter how sympathetic they might be personally.

Besides, the prevailing mood of America after the war was: "We must rebuild Japan and Germany—to make sure they oppose Communism." Since there was no apparent threat of Communism in the Philippines America took the country's political stability for granted, and poured all its money and attention into Japan.

A sore point which was to result in a great deal of resentment against the United States (and provide fuel for the anti-U.S. nationalists) was America's preferential postwar treatment of Japan. In both financial aid and political concern, Japan was given top priority. Japan was seen as a country which must be successfully built up into an economically viable country, to offset the possible temptations of Communism. The results of this sort of priority showed up in mute testimony in the World Trade Fair held a decade following the war. An entire floor was devoted to the enormous range of products from Japan. One single booth held all the Philippines could offer.

The only "free and open society" in southeast Asia, the Philippines drifted on an apparently inexorable downhill run in the immediate postwar years, while its neighbors, Japan, Taiwan, Singapore, flourished in the postwar boom. While America poured money into Japan and India and (after 1949) Taiwan, the Philippines was left to flounder in its newly won independence.

It was not unreasonable that many Filipinos began to wonder: What might have happened if the Americans had never come? Would we have been better off?

What if Admiral Dewey's ships hadn't happened to be in Hong Kong harbor when America decided to go to war with Spain? What if the Americans had never entered Manila, disguised as allies, to steal the Philippines's revolution against Spain?

President McKinley had been convinced that if the United States had not protected the islands, they would have fallen prey to some other big power.

And perhaps they would. Or, winning their independence from Spain, they might have survived. Japan survived. Thailand survived. Both prospered immediately following World War II. Today they are far in advance of the Philippines.

No foreign country colonized Japan. Or Thailand. They were allowed to develop independently, and to achieve —and maintain—a national identity untainted by western influence, unlike the Asian countries that were colonized by the English, the Dutch, the French, and the Americans.

The Philippines certainly would not have been attacked, then defeated, occupied, and destroyed by the Japanese if American bases and America's military might had not been on Philippine soil.

Filipinos had much to ponder in the postwar years as they watched their neighbors, their former foe Japan, and the other countries of southeast Asia who had cooperated with Japan or surrendered to it steadily prosper, while the Philippines, the only country in Asia which had fought for, and with, America, went steadily downhill.

6

The Struggling
Democracy

The economic and social development of the Philippines in the immediate postwar years accentuated rather than mitigated against the enormous disparity between the rich and the poor and did little to create a stable middle class. With shortages in every item—from such basic necessities as daily rice through long dreamed-of luxuries—the moment Filipinos got any money in their hands they began to buy abroad, with the result that imports were soon doubling exports, and inflation was inevitable.

The post-occupation shortages in food, clothing, medical supplies, drugs, electronics, and the like also encouraged the development of wholesale smuggling—a business so eminently profitable that it involved the most powerful, and so well protected that it was beyond the pale of government attack.

Another demoralizing side effect of the war years that resulted from the presence of the United States liberation forces in the Philippines was the creation of a flourishing black market in war supplies, which gave birth to its quota of instant millionaires, both Filipino and American, and giant scandals. In an openhanded gesture, aimed at offering some additional financial aid to the new Philippine republic, the United States, which had amassed quantities of military matériel on Philippine soil in preparation for a possible invasion of Japan, decided it was not practicable to ship all the stuff home and gave the lot—estimated conservatively at over $200 million worth of equipment—to the Philippine government. Handled by the United States military personnel, who wanted nothing so much as to wind up the war details and go home, the stockpile of military goods was dissipated through thefts and scandalous sales to "friends," to the extent that the Philippine government never recovered more than one-fifth of its total paper value.

None of this massive financial wheeling and dealing filtered down to the ninety percent of the population which was still reeling from the moral trauma and physical devastation of the occupation years. It did, however, take its toll on the political front: setting a pattern of cynicism and selfishness among the politicians which was to haunt subsequent administrations. The going philosophy of the postwar Philippines was "anything goes," "to each his own," "everything has a price."

In a period which should have been one of moral exhilaration and selfless efforts at progress for the infant republic, the political structure, rather than providing the necessary democratic push and spirit, seemed on the contrary to impede progress. Besides the combined inherent problems of a war-torn economy, the country's annual natural disasters, and a basic colonial structure which in itself takes years to alter, the checks and balances of the democratic system seemed consistently to produce a stalemate rather than serve to implement needed developments. With the Congress invariably going one direction and the president another, the administration in power could never prove whether its programs were essentially good or bad, nor take responsibility for them, since their aims were seldom realized.

Since neither of the two major parties—the *Nacionalistas* and the *Liberals*—had clear ideological platforms, elections became personality contests, with the people voting for the man they hoped would help them, despite his party affiliations. For neither party represented the interests of the majority. Both were controlled by the caciques—the combination of wealthy business owners and wealthy landowners without whose help, financial and political, no candidate could hope to be elected. While the presidents themselves, from Quezon on, were not born into this same money-aristocracy, they were dependent on it to be elected. A glance at the platforms proclaimed by the six presidents who were elected from the time the Philippines became independent in 1946 until 1972, when the country was placed under martial law, shows that all these men were quite aware of the basic needs of their country and did have ideas for solving them. They were each one elected with the aid of the ruling elite, however, who assumed—and usually correctly —that once a candidate was in office he could be controlled, either personally or through Congress which was also dominated by the same vested interest groups that controlled the political parties.

The democratic concept of "free enterprise" in itself seemed to backfire in the Philippine setting. In imitation of the American system, the Filipinos adopted the policy of free enterprise and limited government interference.

In an effort to stimulate business growth and hopefully reduce the alarming rate of unemployment in the immediate postwar years, the government also went into large-scale deficit financing and easy credit. This, however, only resulted in a succession of unbalanced national budgets, a national deficit, and skyrocketing inflation as imports regularly outdistanced exports. As prices of commodities soared, and reform tax and land legislation continued to meet instant death in Congress, the majority who had elected their leaders in good faith—and hope—became increasingly restless and disenchanted—especially in the provinces where peasant farmers (until 1973) were earning no more than $500 per year. For each new political scandal, or each new rise in food costs, there was a fresh flock of peasant farmers receptive to the blandishments of the strong and growing Communist movements.

It was a threatening political situation of which the Philippine presidents were not unaware. The unrest was always there, boiling just beneath the surface of Philippine political life, erupting periodically into armed revolts. During President Quezon's administration the farmers around Laguna and Cavite in Luzon staged the bloody Sakdal revolt, after which Quezon, who recognized their legitimate grievances, considered the division of land held by the big landowners—a project which was cut short by the outbreak of the war.

During President Roxas's administration land reform was again under consideration. Roxas had become personally acquainted with the shocking inequities and helplessness of the tenants through his wife, who with her family had large land holdings in the province of Bulacan. Seeing the need of appropriate legislation to protect tenants against the possible tyranny and abuse of landowners, Roxas outlined a Tenancy Act. While not a true land reform bill, this act, which he did succeed in getting through Congress, offered some legal recourse to tenants where previously there had been none.

"Landlessness" has always been the source of Communist strength in the Philippines. Throughout the basically agrarian country no more than ten percent of the farmers who work the land have ever owned the land they work. In Pampanga, in central Luzon, heart of the Socialist and Communist movements in the islands, only nine percent of the rich rice and sugar lands are owned by the peasant farmers.

The two dominant forces in the lives of the Philippine peasants are the Church, which controls their spiritual existence, and the landlord who controls their material life. Callous landowners were often abetted in their economic subjugation of the peasants by unscrupulous priests who sidled with the elite against the needs or grievances of the peasants. It was this coalition in particular which furnished an active breeding ground for Communism in the provinces. Ideologues of both the Socialist and Communist parties were always able to put together a formidable farmers' army drawn from this group. That this mass base of Communist support represents economic and social deprivation more than it does political ideology is a fact well known to most Filipino leaders but given little credence by outsiders.

The American advisors to the Philippine presidents immediately following World War II viewed the Philippine farmers' uprisings and farmers' armies—especially the "People's Army against the Japanese," the Huks—as totally Communist, and urged a strong-arm approach to the problem on the part of the Philippine government which would outlaw Communism and subjugate Communist groups with military force.

There is little doubt that had the Huks succeded in overthrowing the Philippine government, as they came very close to doing in 1951, there would have been a clear Communist take-over in the Philippines. However, the mass base of the Communist forces cannot be so neatly defined. In the late 1920s the farmers' labor organization gave birth to the agrarian socialist party. It is at this point that Luis Taruc, son of a Pampanga peasant, emerged as a leader in the Socialist party. Then, in 1932, when the Communist party was banned in the Philippines, the Russian-oriented Philippine Communists merged with the Socialists. In 1941 this group enlisted the support of the peasants to form the "People's Army against the Japanese," the Huks. The leaders included both former Socialists, like Taruc, and Communists. But the mass base were peasant farmers. When their leaders were hunted down and arrested by the Americans at the time of liberation, and then later, when their representatives were refused seats in Congress, the Huks became angry and militant, and open to persuasion by the Communist ideologues that the only answer was to overthrow the existing government which the farmers had become convinced represented only the interests of the hated landowners.

By 1948, the Huks had assembled an army estimated in number at 30,000 people which had, according to the Huk "Supremo," their military leader Luis Taruc's claim at that time, "a million sympathizers" who aided and protected the Huks against sporadic forays by the government forces.

At first there was only token effort on the part of the

Philippine army to war with the Huks. With no clear leadership from the top, and no sense of real and impending danger, the Philippine soldiers would go out into the rural areas, "fire a few shots in the air," claim casualties, and send in a report to appease the administration. A disinterested and demoralized fighting force, the military often abused the barrio people, with the result that the peasants became more and more alienated from the government and protective of the Huks in their midst. Taruc's estimate of a million sympathizers was no idle boast.

In 1948 President Roxas died suddenly of a heart attack while still in office, and his vice-president, Elpidio Quirino, became president. Although Roxas had yielded to United States pressures, he was at the same time a strong and relatively forceful leader on the home front who had managed to keep hold of the reins of government. Quirino, on the contrary, while personally a man of intelligence and sensitivity who derived from a humble background and understood the problems of the poor, did not have the fortitude to withstand the mounting pressures of political corruption, and he became a victim of his associates. Although he personally was uncorruptible, his administration was soon characterized by wholesale corruption. Tax evasion was so routine that it is estimated the government collected no more than twenty-five percent of its taxes. The treasury became so depleted that government employees were owed back pay and the public works program had to be stopped. While a few persons were making fortunes, the mass of people were sinking to even lower depths of poverty: a perfect setup for a Communist take-over.

Quirino was not ignorant of the building threat. In an

effort to defuse the growing tension, he made an offer of amnesty to the Huks and attempted to negotiate with them. Luis Taruc came out of the hills for a meeting, but no agreement was reached and the Huks were once again outlawed and the military ordered to search them out and kill them. Landowners began forming their own private armies under the guise of defense against the Huks.

In 1949 Quirino ran for election with the support of the *Liberal* party. The *Nacionalistas'* candidate, José Laurel, launched a savage attack on the corruption of the Quirino administration. The Liberals took up the cudgels —literally, in the forms of goon squads, vote buying, and voter intimidation—with the result the 1949 campaign was labeled the "dirtiest and bloodiest" in Philippine history. During the fracas several hundred people were killed, and the election results (which kept Quirino in office) were considered so questionable that it was said "even the birds and the bees voted," the dead voted once and the living more than once.

The barrio people were so disgusted that many more flocked to the Huks. By 1950 the Huk People's Army of Liberation was physically and psychologically ready to overthrow the Quirino government (and its "American advisers") and set up a "people's government." By now the Huks had worked out a sophisticated sub rosa network of quasi-governmental administration of their own. They levied taxes in the provinces, which, along with occasional raids on landowners, succeeded in filling their treasury. Firearms and ammunition were no problem to acquire in the postwar Philippines, if one had the money, and their troops were better trained, equipped, and disciplined than the Philippine militia.

It was at this point that the United States belatedly

turned the full force of its attention to what was going on in the Philippines. Philippine expert Colonel Edward Geary Lansdale, who had served in U.S. Army Intelligence in the Pacific theater, got the message across in Washington that the Philippines was threatened with an imminent Communist take-over. Lansdale, who had spent several years in the Philippines, not only knew the island barrios and the Huks; he also knew the one man who might be able to do something to stop them.

Since the ogre of a Communist take-over was a threat to both American bases and American business interests, it was not difficult at this juncture to win America's attention and financial support.

Word flew to Manila, via the American advisers to President Quirino, to appoint Representative Ramon Magsaysay as his Secretary of Defense, to take over the problem of stopping the Huk rebellion.

Magsaysay himself was not unknown to the United States military. A native of the province of Zambales, in western Luzon, the big, burly, blunt spoken young man had been the superintendent of his father-in-law's bus company at the outbreak of World War II, at which time he joined and served with the American forces. After Japan moved into the Philippines, Magsaysay was sent by the Americans back to his home province to help organize a resistance group there.

Following the war he was a natural choice to become a candidate for the House of Representatives from his district in the country's first free election. In Congress he became the House's chairman of the National Defense Committee and went to Washington in 1949 to plead the cause of benefits for Filipino veterans. It was there, that year, that he became acquainted with, or perhaps re-

acquainted with, Colonel Lansdale. In Lansdale's esti-
mation, the rangy, honest, outspoken Magsaysay, a "man
of the people," of obvious personal strength and courage,
who had already shown himself cooperative and loyal to
the American forces, was a perfect choice to be the
"white knight" to lead the Philippines out of the dangers
of Communism, and set her on the road to freedom and
American-style democracy.

And, in fact, the combination of Magsaysay's Lincoln-
esque qualities and knowledge and sympathy with barrio people, coupled with Lansdale's shrewd understanding of psychological warfare, did prove a lethal and effective temporary answer to the Communist threat.

The "mystery man" of Philippine politics (who is said
to be the prototype of Colonel Hillandale in *The Ugly
American*), Lansdale first surfaced in Asia as an intelligence officer in the Pacific theater in World War II. In
the Philippines at the end of the war, Lansdale chose to
stay on until 1948, after which he returned to Washington. In 1950 he was sent back to the Philippines to "advise," or, more correctly, mastermind the government
fight against Communist overthrow. One can find the
American official view of the Philippine situation at the
time of the Huk rebellion in Lansdale's memoir (*In the
Midst of Wars*, Major General Edward Geary Lansdale,
U.S.A.F., retired) which details some of his personal role
in America's fight against Communism in Asia, both in
the Philippines and Vietnam.

A true disciple of the foreign policy later made official
by John Foster Dulles, Colonel Lansdale saw the Huk
movement only as an attempted Communist take-over of
the Philippines, a war of ideologies between Communism
and democracy. He defined the Huk resistance army as

"a guerrilla organization founded in March 1942 by the Communist party of the Philippines for the avowed patriotic purpose of fighting against the Japanese forces then occupying the Philippines."

In Lansdale's view, the "basic cause" of the Huk rebellion was "impatience of . . . Communist leaders to gain control of the Philippines." It is also interesting to note that Lansdale refers to the Philippine agrarian code of that time as a "model of enlightened social thinking" and the age-old familiar cry of "land for the landless" as a mere Communist slogan.

According to Lansdale's account, the peasants protected the Huks because they had become embittered by the corruption of the Quirino administration.

In actual fact, much of the bitterness which led to the mass support of the Huks in the provinces can be attributed to the treatment of the Huks by the American forces when the Philippines was liberated. Ignoring the role of the People's Army as a resistance force against the Japanese, the U.S. Army Counterintelligence Corps, acting on the premise that the Huks were all Communists, rounded up and imprisoned their leaders in 1945, and then attempted to disarm the farmers' army. The Huk leaders were eventually released and in 1946 seven of them, including Luis Taruc, were elected to the first Congress of the new republic. President Roxas, yielding to American pressure, refused to recognize them and had them unseated on charges of "fraud" and corruption. The Americans did not want Communists recognized in the Philippine government and did not want their voice in Congress when the constitutional amendment granting American parity rights with Filipinos was up for vote.

It was at this point, discounted as patriots and spurned

in their efforts to participate in the government by peaceful means, that the embittered Huks withdrew to the hills, retrenched, and began mounting a massive resistance army designed to overthrow the pro-American government and install a government "of the people."

As Secretary of Defense, with full financial and advisory backing from America, Magsaysay launched a brilliant counterattack against the Huks. Reversing the "kill the Huks" policy of previous years, Magsaysay reorganized and revitalized the Philippine army to make it provide a liaison between the government and the people in the provinces. He threw in the constabulary (the Philippine national police) to beef up the army to 50,000 men, then put them under tight discipline. Atrocities were reported and punished. Soldiers carried not only arms but offers of amnesty and promises of aid to the impoverished farmers. Magsaysay himself oversaw the entire operation, popping up in barrios without advance notice, a symbol of goodwill and help to the barrio people.

His greatest coup was when he managed to infiltrate the Communist group sufficiently to discover the whereabouts of the politburo in Manila, then swooped down on the Communist ringleaders, imprisoning them all, just as the Huk army ringed Manila. Leaderless and rudderless, the masses of farmer-soldiers fell back to the hills. At this point Magsaysay used his army as a citizen's army to aid the rehabilitation and resettlement of the poor and disenfranchised peasants on the barrio level. The Huk army gradually broke up into splinter factions as many ex-Huks accepted the government offer of amnesty. Even Taruc finally accepted the white flag and personally surrendered to the representatives of Magsaysay in 1954, accepted his offer of amnesty—which in his case was reneged, and Taruc was imprisoned, where he remained for the next fourteen years.

With their rebellion successfully squelched and many of their numbers accepting Magsaysay's offer of amnesty, the Huks nonetheless continued to operate as a political body smoldering beneath the surface of Philippine politics. After their defeat the Huk leaders split on ideological issues and the young activists, led by Amado Guerrero, the nom de guerre of Jose Sison, who was said to have received his political indoctrination in China, reorganized the Philippine Communist party along the principles of Mao Tse Tung and formed the New Peoples Army based in northern Luzon.

On the heels of his stunning victory over the Huks, Magsaysay resigned his job as Secretary of Defense and prepared to run for the presidency. Switching from Quirino's *Liberal* party to the *Nacionalistas,* he gained strong support from ex-guerrillas, the Catholic Church, and, perhaps most importantly, the United States press. His friend and mentor, Colonel Lansdale, who had been, before his military career, an ad man in San Francisco, threw all the ingenuity of the American media to the task of "making a president." Big, rugged, honest, and friendly, Magsaysay was a natural for the billing of the "Lincoln of the Philippines." He could wade through Philippine backcountry mud barefoot without a grimace, eat sticky rice with his fingers, fix a stalled car engine, throw his big shoulders against the back of a recalcitrant jeep, or kiss brown babies—as the political stumping required.

There was talk of CIA money in the campaign. But whether or not dollars did change hands, there was no

doubt that Magsaysay was America's darling—the first
Filipino to receive totally favorable coverage by the
United States press. During the tense period when there
was some question as to whether the embittered President Quirino, who apparently felt "had" by the American
advisers who had urged him to take such an asp to the
bosom of his cabinet, would relinquish his office to his
former Secretary without a fight, an American man-of-
war stood by in the Manila harbor ready to whisk Magsaysay to safer territory in case there was an armed conflict.

That Quirino felt "taken" by the whole Magsaysay deal
is apparent by his order to his ambassador in Washington to tell Secretary of State Dulles that Colonel Lansdale was hereafter to be declared persona non grata in
the Philippines—a message which Dulles managed to
avoid receiving. Later the matter got lost in the election
excitement, with the result that Lansdale stayed on—although the President's brother is said to have taken a few
potshots at him and some of the leaders of the Liberal
party pressed for an investigation of his meddling into
Philippine politics.

While Magsaysay was eminently suited to the purposes
of the American foreign policy of that period, he does
not, in the long view, emerge as the best of all possible
presidents of the Philippines. The least equipped intellectually and politically, his problems began to emerge
as soon as he took office. A good hand-shaking cam-
paigner, Magsaysay did not have the patience or experience for the office work of the presidency, nor the
ability to delegate authority. Desirous of being a true
hero, all men to all people, he threw open the palace for

"everyman's" complaints, tried to see to every noxious detail personally, and would fly off, at a moment's notice, to all parts of the country.

A breath of fresh country air and a symbol of freedom for the little man, Magsaysay emerges as perhaps more important as a symbol than an executive. Although he had no trouble getting American funding to wage his fight against Communism, the Americans who had created a democratic Philippine president had not made any similar inroads in the Philippine Congress, which was just as firmly entrenched as in former years. Magsaysay's social welfare programs, in which he passionately believed, scarcely got off the ground for lack of support in Congress, and his successor, his vice-president, Carlos Garcia, was forced to cut them off entirely for lack of funds. Magsaysay did succeed in setting up a farmers' cooperative, and he did establish an Agricultural Tenancy Act which was designed to break up large land holdings and gave the government the authority to buy up large estates and make them available for purchase by the tenants—a plan which could have done much to ease the agrarian problem, except that there was no funding for it.

Magsaysay's Congress, made up principally of men of the landlord class, was completely unsympathetic to the President's democratic desires and refused to legislate or implement his pet bills. Magsaysay, a man of action, is said to have once commented, in head-shaking frustration, "I can go out to the people and get a majority of four to one at any time. Yet I can't get a majority of one in the Senate!"

His plan for the rehabilitation and resettlement of the former Huk guerrillas also came up against some hard realities. It was true that the large island of Mindanao was unexploited and underpopulated. It was, however, populated by the Muslims who, without modern titles to their land, nonetheless felt that it all belonged to them by ancestral right. As Christian Filipino settlers moved in from Luzon, the Muslims began to fight back, convinced they were being encroached upon. There was also the problem that merely providing a spot of land for the landless had little meaning unless the land was also accompanied with such necessities for its development as rural credit (to buy implements, animals, seed, fertilizer, etc.), roads, power supplies, and water. (It was estimated that when the Japanese were finally driven out of the islands eighty percent of the country's water supplies were left polluted.)

Although the area where the Muslims are congregated, the large island of Mindanao and neighboring Sulu, represents thirty-four percent of the total land surface of the Philippine archipelago, the Muslim Filipinos had never felt that they were part of the government in Luzon, nor that their interests were represented by that government. At the time that Philippine independence was being considered in the United States Congress in 1935, some Muslim Filipino leaders, inspired by American "imperialists," notified the United States Congress that they did not want the islands of Mindanao and Sulu to be included in the agreement, since they feared their lands would then be seized and taken away from them by the Christian Filipinos.

While the Muslim problem is more complex than simply land ownership, embracing as it does religious and cultural conflicts as well, land nonetheless is a major part of the prickly overall problem. Settled before the rest of the Philippines was Christianized by the Spanish, the Muslim Philippines was developed into a feudal society which was ruled by chieftains. They considered all the land in the southern islands as Muslim land held in common by the reigning sultans. None of the Muslims held any title to these lands which they lived on, and there was no concept in the Muslim tradition of either the purchase or sale of land.

When the Christian settlers began moving into Mindanao the local rulers, the *datus*, accepted their money for land, allowed them to clear and cultivate it, and then, likely as not, when the land looked prosperous the *datu* wanted it back. If the Christian settler refused, there was apt to be a bloody conflict. In the Muslim mind the lands remained ancestral lands and did not belong to the Christians, even if they had settled there. In areas where the expanding Christian community eventually outnumbered the Muslims, the Muslims were gradually forced back until they relinquished their claims and moved back to uncultivated lands.

As waves of Christian settlers kept coming, drawn by the rich resources—the forests, mines, agricultural and grazing lands—the Muslims were beaten back further and further, so that by 1960 they had been reduced to a minority population with minority holdings, and only two provinces left in their command.

But wherever they did remain, the Muslims continued to fight the Christian encroachment, just as they had fought for their existence against the Spanish and the Americans.

Although President Magsaysay had no problem getting government aid from America earmarked to fight Communists, American investment money was still not forthcoming to the Philippines. The Philippine government appeared too insecure and unstable to attract major investment. "Smart" money was going instead into "stabilized" authoritarian governments such as Thailand and Singapore, Indonesia and Taiwan. Nor, with America's political backing, could the Philippines attract aid or investment money from other countries. Australia, Canada, and the United Kingdom were "a different club" with their own set of dependents. And no Socialist country was going to get interested in an American satellite during the days of the cold war between the United States and the U.S.S.R.

Always patently pro-American and dependent, in his executive decisions, on his American advisers (his "ghost" speech writer was also an American), President Magsaysay disagreed with the views of his own foreign minister, the experienced and knowledgeable former lawyer, Secretary of Foreign Affairs Carlos Garcia, who was concurrently Magsaysay's vice president. Garcia, who had participated in the founding of the United Nations and the Southeast Asia Treaty Organization, saw the Philippines's future position as one in which the coun try would increasingly side with the fraternity of Asian nations, with less and less dependence, politically and economically, on the United States. But when Garcia came out with an "Asia for Asians" policy for the Philippines Magsaysay—who believed that the Philippines should always side with the United States, even against its Asian neighbors—denounced it.

In March 1957 President Magsaysay was killed in a plane crash at Cebu, eight months short of finishing his first term in office. Garcia became president. There was talk of sabotage, but no evidence was ever uncovered. It was just one more of the frequent fatal accidents that occur in a country where air is the principal means of transportation between islands and blinding tropical storms blow in with lightning swiftness.

Also a guerrilla leader (and even better known as such than his predecessor), the new President promised the grieved and stricken people that he would carry on in Magsaysay's footsteps. A very different sort of man— quiet where Magsaysay was voluble, older by twelve years, a lawyer by training, Garcia had none of the heroic charm of Magsaysay, a fact the rather shy and self-contained man was only too well aware of. He also enjoyed none of the adulation given his predecessor by the American press. He was, in fact, made a target for vilification by *Time* magazine, which had done much to elect Magsaysay. In the next election, however, in the fall of 1957, Garcia carried the day and got his own turn at the presidential table, winning out over five candidates, who included the anti-American nationalist Recto and former President Quirino's brother.

The political dark horse who emerged into public prominence in this election was Diosdado Macapagal, who came out of nowhere to neatly win the vice-presidency for the Liberal party. From a family of tenant farmers in Pampanga (home of the Huks), Macapagal was one of the few ex-peasants who broke those chains entirely by his own efforts, working his way up, supporting himself throughout his school years, and becoming a lawyer, then a politician. A slender, handsome man with startlingly light-ringed dark eyes in a narrow-featured, Malay face, Macapagal knew the plight of the peasants from personal experience, as did few who gained high elective office. President Garcia, who was not pleased at the idea of having a vice-president from the opposition party, chose to ignore his new vice-president and give him no tasks, with the result that Macapagal used his time to personal political advantage by stumping the countryside. By 1961 he was so well known and well liked that he won the presidential election handily, getting the same mass support from the people that had elected Magsaysay.

But when he moved into the presidential chair, he may have doubted the wisdom of his political ambition. The national debt at this point was nearly one billion dollars. The treasury was empty. Unemployment was rampant. The new President stated his goals: end the corruption which still haunted the government; improve the rice/corn production (a rice-eating nation, the Philippines had one of the lowest rice production records in Asia, and never grew enough to feed its own population); lure foreign investment with a new socio-economic program aimed at developing local industry and increasing employment. And, first and foremost, tackle the long overdue problem of a genuine, viable land reform program.

An indefatigable worker who well understood the basic needs of the country, Macapagal came up with some excellent programs, including the first full-scale land reform bill—then tried to get them through Congress.

When he was faced with the usual stalemate of landed interests resisting all change, the energetic President tried to get politicians to switch parties in order to develop a working majority for the Liberal party, which he felt he might influence to get his pet bills through. The reaction to these efforts was, from the political front, the accusation of "dictatorship" and efforts to "destroy the two-party system." On the level of the people he was trying to help, the reaction was disenchantment as they waited in vain for the legislation the new President had promised.

Macapagal was a good administrator and a knowledgeable executive whose aims and programs were appropriate for the orderly development of the country. But his plans were, in the main, blocked by Congress. His epochal land reform bill finally got passed in an emasculated form in 1963, but had so little teeth to it that no visible gains were felt during his administration. The important paragraph which provided for the actual implementation of the program had been excised. ("It was like giving you a car without gasoline," explained Secretary of Agrarian Reform Conrado Estrella.) Finally, his administration was tarnished by threatened impeachment proceedings arising from a scandal which involved an American ex-GI, Harry Stonehill, whose questionable activities had been protected from investigation during both the Garcia and Macapagal administrations (although not by either of the presidents personally). The impeachment idea was dropped and no one doubted Macapagal's personal honesty, but his popularity had waned and the stage was set for another "new face" to fight the apparently insurmountable problems of getting the Philippines on the road to recovery and prosperity.

In 1965 Macapagal ran for reelection and was defeated. The new face this time—on which the faltering nation chose to pin its hopes—was the former president of the Senate, another lawyer and experienced politician, and the most famous ex-guerrilla of them all: Ferdinand E. Marcos. Charismatic in his own right, the trim, athletic, forceful candidate had as his "secret weapon" his wife Imelda Ramualdez Marcos—a statuesque beauty with massive amounts of shining black hair; round, dark eyes; a warm, feminine manner; and a pleasing soprano singing voice which she used to political advantage during the campaign, singing solos or duets with her husband. A former local beauty queen from Leyte, Imelda Marcos showed poise, grace, and also, early on, a natural talent and zest for politics. The most glamorous political pair the Philippines had produced, the Marcoses aroused the sort of romantic excitement which the young Kennedys inspired in the United States.

Each election the Filipino people enthusiastically cast their votes for the most appealing candidate—the long-awaited "strong man" who could lead them to the promised land of change and progress. Despite repeated disappointments with administrations, there was always election excitement. The people's disenchantment set in later when nothing got done, and all the fine-sounding election promises died aborning.

Characteristically, in the 1965 election Filipinos were looking for another *datu*, a strong father figure. And apparently they sensed that they found this in Marcos (as they had once found it in Magsaysay). A rather slightly built, lean, muscular man with small, taut features and glittering, dark eyes in an impassive face, Marcos was already established in the popular imagination as a hero figure of proven physical courage. He was the most decorated for bravery of all Filipino guerrillas. An astute lawyer (who had once successfully defended himself in a murder charge) and an able senator, he was also a well-read man and an avid student of history, with a strong sense of personal destiny which transmitted to his audiences. Self-contained, steely, confident, Marcos had the deadly calm of the poker player who never gives away his hands, who knows how to wait. It was a honed and complex personality but an unquestionably strong one. One that appealed to the need for leadership from the mass of Filipinos, judging by the landslide victory. Marcos, who had switched from the Liberal to the Nacionalista party to run for the presidency, won by an overwhelming seventy-five percent. For vice-president, he got the Nacionalistas' Fernando Lopez, a member of one of the country's most powerful and wealthiest families who own controlling interests in communications, sugar, commerce, and shipping. (The Lopezes had been charged by President Macapagal in 1963 with using their family power to control the economic and political life of the country.) For a Congress, Marcos drew a mixed bag, weighted in favor of the opposition. The *Liberals* gained control of the House, the Senate was divided.

The country had voted in a new "hero." But once again it looked like the usual stalemate: a fresh face in the same tired setting—a president with a reform program pitted against an oligarchic vice-president and Congress.

The country was, despite Macapagal's efforts at salvage, still suffering from an economic hiatus. Poverty and unemployment were rampant. Crime and smuggling were on the increase. Nearly twenty-five percent of the labor force was unemployed or underemployed, with unemployment increasing at an annual rate of three percent (about the same as the spiraling population). The national per capita income was around $600 a year.

The government coffers were dangerously low. In 1962 President Macapagal had tried to reverse the trend by introducing a policy of decontrol, to lower imports and improve the deficit. But by 1965 the Philippines was teetering on the verge of bankruptcy. Only emergency first aid from a consortium of twelve American banks, in the form of a $40 million loan, had saved the country from bankruptcy.

Marcos came in with an impressive slate of campaign promises: stop importing rice; increase rice production; hold food prices down; eradicate smuggling; lower crime and unemployment; implement the land reform program. Recognizing the value of his predecessor's impressive attack on agrarian unrest, Marcos ordered the land reform program resurrected, refurbished, and put into action.

But by 1967 Marcos had not been able to implement many of his proposals, due to opposition from landowners and the lawyers of landowners. What few land transfers had been attempted had ended up in the courts in a legal contest.

And the Huk movement was beginning to build up again. In a report made by the Senate Committee on Defense in April 1967 Senator Manuel Manahan reported:

"The Huks are now . . . running a sort of 'invisible government' in Pampanga, in the western sector of Bulacan and in the southern fringes of Nueva Ecija and Tarlac. Their intensive fund raising operations have assumed scandalous proportions. . . . the unholy alliance between the Huks and government officials is a downright mockery of our democratic system. . . .

". . . there is reason to believe that the Huk movement is in large measure an agrarian reform movement. Although the Huk leaders are either communist or have communist leanings, the rank and file of the organization is made up of . . . landless tenants who do not know the difference between democracy and communism. . . . it is the peasants' hunger for land which is [being] exploited by the communists."

In 1968, the British-educated Swedish economist Raymond Nelson concluded his study of the Philippines (in a book of that name) with this rhetorical question:

"Will President Marcos rise above partisan politics and carry out the essential reforms so badly needed by his country? The results of the elections leave him with little excuse. In the short time left before the presidential election in 1969 he must work hard to restore the confidence of the people. For the sake of the nation he must urge the members of both political parties to sink their differences and devote their energies to eliminating poverty, nepotism, smuggling, and crime. He must de-centralize parts of the administration, free the civil service from political interference, improve transportation, communication and power facilities, and take heed of the grievances of the forgotten tribal minorities, many of whom are exploited by unscrupulous local officials and land-grabbers. . . ."

In his first term, 1965–1969, President Marcos had not been able to implement many of his ideas for reform. As a result, the people were once again becoming restive. Dissidence was rising. Subversive groups were gaining fresh recruits. The Maoists had transferred their base of military activities to northern Luzon, where they were building up their New People's Army to launch fresh attacks against the government forces. Outbreaks of fighting between Christians and Muslims in Mindanao were on the increase.

Yet, judging by the results of the 1969 election, in which Marcos, the first Philippine president since Quezon to be reelected, won by a handsome two million majority, the mass of Filipinos still believed that, given another chance, Marcos might make good his promises.

7

The New Society

When President Marcos declared martial law in September 1972, the Philippine republic, for the first time since its birth in 1946, had the opportunity to discover whether an individual administration's programs for the country were or were not beneficial. With the stumbling block of congressional action removed and programs implemented directly by presidential decree, there was no one to blame but the President himself and his handpicked cabinet if anything went wrong.

For the outsider, the immediately puzzling thing about the Philippines under martial law is, Why aren't the people complaining more about their loss of civil liberties? One quick answer to that lies in the structure of society which still obtains: there are people who complain vociferously, but they represent only a very small fraction of the populace. To the mass base of Filipinos civil liberties—which were often hostage to the whim of a warlord or landlord—are hardly relevant. Far more important are the pressing problems of food, land, and employment.

There is also the question of Filipino martial law as opposed to the strong-arm martial law of, say, Greece or Spain or Chile. In contrast to martial law elsewhere, even the tartest critics, if they personally view it at all, must admit the Philippine version is relatively benign. (*The New York Times,* which is editorially opposed to the Marcos martial law, nonetheless judges it "mild.") No one is getting roughed up. No one is getting killed. The military is under the firm control of civilian authority and is rarely visible. For the average person on the street in Manila the atmosphere is far more peaceful than it was prior to the confiscation of private firearms, when many more weapons were visible in the hands of private citizens than are now visible in the hands of the constabulary. The reassuring aura of peace and order is reflected in the spiraling rate of tourism (thirty percent above last year, with Manila hotels enjoying ninety percent occupancy).

Total crime is down forty-nine percent (murder seventy-five percent). The relation of nighttime hours to criminal activity was shown at the time of the referendum vote in August 1973, when the curfew (which had originally been imposed to keep urban Communist guerrillas from moving arms at night) was temporarily lifted and street crime promptly reasserted itself, spiraling thirty percent in the three free nights.

There is grumbling, especially among the elite, about travel restrictions, about enforced land division, about the boring one-sided press. Several leaders of the wealthiest and most powerful families, such as Eugenio Lopez (brother of the former vice-president) fled the country and established their financial beachheads elsewhere. Many individual Filipino fortunes are now resting in banks in San Francisco, New York, and Geneva.

In Manila some of the lack of antipathy to martial law may also be laid to the personality of the head of the constabulary, who is responsible for carrying out the military restrictions, Brigadier General Fidel Ramos. The man in the highest military position, who would be in line to run the country if there should be a military coup, Ramos is, due to his own restrained personality and erudition, acceptable to the intellectuals as well as the administration.

The most pressing question to both Filipinos and foreigners is succession. Who would take over the reins of government (and continue the President's program) if anything happened to Marcos? The ordinary man on the street assumes there would be a military coup and that General Ramos or another of the generals would become head of the government. Many of the upper class professionals agree. "The generals will have to do it to protect themselves," argued a wealthy lawyer. "Otherwise they would be subject to court martial. They will have to do it to save themselves."

There are several likely possibilities for succession within the President's cabinet, which contains a number of bright young men among the president's "brain trust," such as his Secretary of Defense, Juan Ponce Enrile, or his Executive Secretary, Alex Melchor, or his Secretary of Finance, Cesar Virata, or the Secretary of Industry, Vicente Paterno.

There is considerable conjecture about the possibility of Imelda Marcos taking on the presidency—an idea the queenly and energetic First Lady firmly denies. While Mrs. Marcos clearly enjoys being involved in all phases of the government, she seems to have carved out special areas of interest for her own activity (the national cultural program; the green revolution; population control) and professes not to know enough about the complexities of economics and politics to be able to handle the top job.

There has also been talk of some arrangement being made for a "caretaker" government, composed of a senior cabinet member and Mrs. Marcos, to hold down the fort in an interim capacity until elections could be held. The President has purportedly promised to set up an executive council to formulate a line of succession.

The President also recently promised (in the fall of 1973) that if all goes well martial law may be lifted next year. In this case the Interim Assembly would convene, the parliamentary form of government provided for by the new constitution would go into effect, and elections would be held for president and prime minister.

When an American reporter chided Marcos for keeping himself in office this long, the President snapped back, "If FDR were still alive, he'd still be your president!"

As is usually true with Marcos, the analogy was not an idle one. He views his "New Society" as a social revolution similar in aim and quality to Franklin Roosevelt's New Deal in 1934, and he is inclined to believe that America might well have faced a bloody revolution from the people if the policies of the previous administration had not been reversed. He clearly believes that the Philippine government would have been overthrown if he had not declared martial law, and through that artificial hiatus been able to put his reform programs into action. As most reformers, Marcos wants to stay in office long enough to see his programs instituted.

I
The Land

One of the first things Marcos did after declaring martial law was to decree the entire country a "land reform area." A student of world history, and a close observer of the progress or lack of it in the Philippines, Marcos saw the land problem, which is shared by most southeast Asian countries,* as integral to the stability of the country, and its solution as the only way to defuse the recurrent threat of a Communist take-over.

Revolution per se does not frighten Marcos. He is himself a "revolutionist" and the apparent *raison d'être* of his New Society is to stage the revolution necessary in the Philippines in a bloodless fashion. In the year since martial law was declared, the major thrust of the President's programs has been to convince the former revolutionaries who would have waged bloody revolution—the students, the peasants, the poor farmers—that the government is going to do it for them.

One of the most significant indices of the effectiveness of this attitude is that Marcos has been able to attract into the workings of the government two of the most militant, and formerly "hunted," revolutionaries in the Philippines: the former Huk military commander Luis Taruc, and the former military commander of the Maoist New People's Army in northern Luzon, Commander "Pusa" (his *nom de guerre,* "the Cat"). If Marcos trips up on his "revolutionary" promises, these two men will

---

* Japan and Taiwan have completed their land reform programs; Malaysia, Sri Lanka (Ceylon), India, and the Philippines are all working on theirs.

drop out of the government fold and fade back to the hills—especially the fiery Pusa, whose NPA soldiers are still out there waiting in northern Luzon.

Commander Pusa, a young, intense, dark-haired man, who was in charge of the Sparrow Unit of the NPA—a unit dedicated to the liquidation of government officials —made it clear that his surrender to the government and cooperation with it has not changed his political views. "We do not want to give the impression that we are no longer communist," he warned. "We believe in Marxism. I will remain a Marxist. But I see that something good is taking place. We are convinced the government is doing what the government would not do before. But, if it stops —we go back to the hills."

Secretary of Defense Enrile, who had once been warned by Senator Aquino that Commander Pusa was out to get him, asked Pusa if indeed this were true. "We came for you twice," Pusa told him. This was part of "Operation MARITES," he explained to Enrile, which was high on the priority list for the NPA and called for the assassination of President Marcos, Information Secretary Tatad, Defense Secretary Enrile, and Chief of Staff Espino.

Taruc, an older, more philosophical, leader than Commander Pusa, is less apt to carry a gun again. But he would not work, as he now does, with the Department of Agrarian Reform if he did not believe the program is being sincerely carried out. "Why shouldn't I be with the government?" he answered the reporter's first, obvious question. "The government is doing what I have fought for all of my life."

A slender, gentle, graying man with the intense gaze of a committed idealist, Taruc sees no contradiction as a former military commander in working with the government. He tried once before, he will remind you, to work "within the system" by peaceful means when he was elected to Congress in 1946. His war on Manila came only after he had been, to his mind, unfairly unseated and his followers outlawed.

At the time he surrendered to Magsaysay, in 1954, Taruc told the President that what the Philippines needed most was a bold land reform program which would abolish tenancy, modernize production, and break the centuries old feudal landlordism whcih kept the nation a backward agricultural economy. Later, from prison, Taruc again warned the Philippine government that "without a militant democratic movement revolution will remain an ever-present possibility and the communists will have their job made easy for them. . . ."

Taruc did not appear concerned about either the much-criticized slowness of the present land program, nor the problems of underfinancing. "If we survived during three and a half years of Japanese occupation and domination— when they were even stealing from us what little food we had—we can weather this," he said emphatically, "for now people have inspiration, hope—in the government and in themselves. And no matter how slow the implementation, the fact that land transfer *is* taking place means that the feudal landowner system is being broken. This gives the farmer a sense of self respect, of security, for the first time. He can see a future for himself and his children."

Various token land reform programs had been on the books in different administrations and the 1963 plan was being implemented—but slowly—under the direction of the Governor of Land Reform Conrado Estrella, during Marcos's first administration. "When martial law was declared," (and the Department of Agrarian Reform established) "it enabled us to force cooperation of landowners and avoid further delays," explained Estrella, and the plan began to accelerate. According to presidential decree, each tenant who qualifies for ownership is awarded from three to five hectares (six and a half to ten and a half acres) of productive rice or corn land. In exchange for the cancellation of old debts relating to the sharecropping of the land, and the acquisition of the land, the farmer is obliged to join a local cooperative which guarantees payments to the owner and provides the supplies of seed, farm implements, and fertilizers. The cooperative also handles the eventual sale of the crop, eliminating a middleman and insuring the farmer a fair price.

To be successful, the program has to reach far past the simple parceling out of land. It must offer a package deal which carries with it adequate provision for credit, technical assistance, irrigation facilities, and even infrastructure—in terms of farm-to-market roads, ports, etc.—which actually amounts to a massive overhauling and modernization of the rural areas. It is estimated that to complete the program properly would require at least a billion-dollar outlay.

To finance the land transfer, President Marcos first organized a Land Bank with $300 million in cash and securities which was provided principally by the Central Bank in exchange for land reform bonds. The original terms of land transfer were ten percent cash to the owner and the remainder in government bonds, or ninety percent could be amortized over a fifteen-year period on the basis of a fixed percent of the normal crop yield.

One of the first major stumbling blocks the government program ran into, in addition to lack of adequate financing, was the size of land holdings. At the outset, when the initial surveying was being done, government officials in charge of the program discovered that there were not as many huge landed estates as had been assumed. Indeed, nearly seventy-five percent of all the landowners owned less than twenty acres of land. Many of these small landowners were not people of enormous wealth but retired military officers and businessmen. Instead of taking all land of 7 hectares (14.5 acres) up as originally scheduled, the government began at the top with the largest holdings from 100 hectares (250 acres) up. After these were distributed, they started on the second tier of lands of over 50 hectares (125 acres). Then they turned to the lands of 25 hectares and above.

Neither the large nor small landowners were satisfied, however, with the method of payment offered by the government. By July 1973, 30,000 land transfers, of the target of one million, had been completed. To speed up the operation, President Marcos gave the land bank broader powers to implement the exchange, and a variety of types of payment was offered—including an opportunity for owners to transform their land holdings into commercial and industrial assets in companies in which the government now held interest.

It was predicted at the time this change was made that the transfers would soon double, which did prove true. By September 1973, 75,000 tenant farmers in sixty-six provinces had received titles to land.

A missing link in the land reform program is the huge sugar plantations. Thus far, land reform has affected only rice and corn lands, and has not touched the big holdings in rubber, coconut, and, most important, sugar. There are several reasons for this. Sugar is the major export product of the Philippines on which the national economy depends, and it is covered by international marketing agreements. The administration is reluctant to risk dislocating the economy. Another reason is that the relationship between landowner and farmer on sugar plantations is not the same at it is in rice and corn lands. The 450,000 sugar workers are not tenant farmers or sharecroppers, as the rice and corn farmers are, but laborers who are covered by minimum-wage laws. The government seems more inclined to woo the sugar barons into self-reformation by prodding from the Department of Labor for higher wages and benefits for laborers than to attempt to break up their holdings. Already, the most powerful sugar group, the Montelibano interests, are spearheading a change in management's attitude to sugar workers, by acknowledging that the future requires that the workers be treated as industrial partners with their own bargaining power, rather than as peasant labor.

An Indian journalist of Socialist leanings, who was recently stationed in Manila, defended the Philippine government's program—even to its hands-off policy toward the sugar interests. "At least President Marcos is trying to elevate the status of the poor," the writer observed. "In India [the only democracy in Asia] the ruling class is still so indifferent to the mass of people that money is appropriated for defense when thousands are starving. Here, the government is aware of the poor and trying to help them."

"It's the fact that land reform *is being done* that is important," Luis Taruc concluded. "It was never done before. And that is what the peoples' armies, the socialist

movement, the communist movement in the Philippines is
all about. When the tenant farmers become owners of the
land, there will be no more attempts to overthrow the
government."

If, indeed, Marcos's land reform program succeeds in
permanently defusing the threat of a Communist overthrow of the Philippine government, that in itself will win
him a respected spot in history, if he accomplishes nothing
else. It is the key to his "revolution," and his administration will stand or fall on its success.

II
The Economy

So far as facts and figures are concerned, the Marcos
New Society's most impressive accomplishments have
been in the economic area, and in attracting foreign investment. One year after the declaration of martial law
and the implementation of the reforms of the New Society, the GNP in real terms had increased 8.7 percent.
Exports had risen an astonishing 54 percent. The national
balance of payments (on a comparative basis for nine
months of January-September 72/73) had shifted dramatically from a $18.2 million deficit to a $441.8 million
surplus—the highest percentage climb enjoyed by any of
the southeast Asian countries. The international reserve,
which had stood at $220 million in September 1972, had
spiraled to $739 million by September 1973, the highest
in Philippine history. Foreign investments had skyrock-
eted 161 percent. The stock market was booming, with
Philippine shares appearing for the first time on inter-

national portfolios. The government had repaired its
credit image so that foreign borrowing was easily
available.*

From the vantage point of "a year later," the clear outlines of the Marcos battle plan begin to emerge. In September 1972, when martial law was declared, the first
thing that had to be done before any reform plans got
under way was to establish peace and order on both of
the two military fronts, in northern Luzon and southern
Mindanao, where fighting was taking place between government forces and insurgents. On the civilian front, the
confiscation of firearms and breaking up of private armies
took care of the menace—with the exception of the Muslims, for whom the request to give up firearms was the
spur to new military activity against the government.
(According to the Muslim code, a man is naked without
a weapon, and the average Muslim would sooner give up
one of his wives than his rifle.) One year later, the fighting in the north, on the Communist front in Isabela, has
been reduced to an occasional foray, and the Communist
threat is now considered a minor one (thanks largely to
the ameliorating effects of the land reform program). In
the south, fighting is still going on, although it is now
sufficiently contained in limited areas of Sulu and Basilan
so that the government's development program for Mindanao is going forward.

---

* In June 1973 a consortium of American banks agreed to renew a $50
million revolving credit line with the Central Bank of the Philippines
because "the external reserve position of the Philippines is at a twenty-
five-year high, there was a trade surplus in the first quarter of 1973
and government tax collections are breaking records." The previous
May the Consultative Group for the Philippines, a group of nations
headed by the World Bank, which examines economic performance and
makes recommendations to donor countries, recommended what is said
to be around $250 million in United States aid.

With peace and order established, the constabulary then turned to help out in the social programs, in civic action in the barrios and towns and countryside, on the construction of roads and bridges, the technical assistance to farmers, and to help with increased food production. Under tight discipline from the top, the constabulary has proved to be a positive force in liaison work between the government and the barrios, carrying the message of government concern which has resulted in civilian cooperation. The fact that the Communists in Isabela have been rendered relatively toothless, and their leaders captured, for example, is directly attributable, according to the governor of that province, to the fact that the Isabela peasants have come round to believing in the government, and have ceased to protect the Communist guerrillas in their midst.

The second line of attack designed to stabilize society was to clean up the bumbling bureaucratic-ridden government itself, which sapped off sizable national reserves. With Congress closed, there were no patrons or protectors left, and the incompetents could be fired and replaced, where necessary, with the technical and administrative talent needed to carry out the plans for creating a New Society.

In cleaning up the civil service, Marcos first fingered those officials in the positions most sensitive in relation to the populace: the ones involved in the dispensation or control of taxes, justice, and law. Proceedings instituted against erring officials in the police force, the Department of Justice, the Bureau of Customs, and the Internal Revenue resulted eventually in the arrest of 340 persons and the dismissal of over a thousand. In the Department of Foreign Affairs 174 "overstaying" personnel were recalled, and with the backing of the new hard line in the palace, the Secretary of Foreign Affairs made an unannounced visit to the consulate in Hong Kong and swept it clean—firing the entire staff of fourteen people and replacing them with competent workers.

The Marcos technocrats had a field day putting their departments to rights after the meddlers had been removed. The Budget Commissioner, Faustino C. Sychangco, faced, for the first time, the opportunity to balance the national budget with the "nightmare of the pork barrel" out of his way—the annual dipping into federal funds carried on by each congressman for so-called public works projects for his district. With martial law, Sychangco was at long last in the enviable position of being able to refuse to release federal funds for any purpose except an item on the national budget.

Among the heads that fell were several judges of the Court of First Instance, at the behest of the Secretary of Justice Vicente Abad Santos, the equivalent of our Attorney General. Another of Marcos's apolitical brain trusters, Abad Santos had been recruited from the State University, where he was Dean of Law. After martial law was declared, he forced the retirement of several corrupt and incompetent judges—including one arbitrary fellow who had ordered the arrest of the Secretary of Justice himself, on "contempt of court" charges. Operating on the theory that "justice delayed is justice denied," Secretary Abad Santos also moved to clean the court dockets which contained cases that had been stacked up for as long as ten years.

A large number of the people dropped from civil service were employees whose corruption or inefficiency had become evident to Finance Secretary Virata. He had been trying to fire them since he took office, with the result that he was so hounded by politicians (who were the patrons of the people he was trying to get rid of) demanding his resignation that he had resorted to the use of a secret office in order to carry on his work. After martial law was declared, Virata happily emerged from hiding to take a personal hand in the firing of 800 employees from the Bureau of Customs and 500 in the Internal Revenue Department.

The three major sources of lost tax revenues lay in personal income taxes, real estate taxes, and through the smuggling of untaxed items. It was estimated that no more than twenty-five percent of the tax money due was actually reaching either local or federal coffers.

To pick up on back income taxes, the government offered tax amnesty in terms of government bonds. Any individual who owed back taxes could buy bonds to the amount of the "hidden (undeclared, untaxed) money" and get off free. Frightened, in the early days of martial law, by the specter of the "Crame Hilton" as Virata jokingly calls the Camp Crame detention camp where some political detainees languished, wealthy Filipinos rushed to accept the offer of amnesty and turn in realistic returns. (Collection from Filipinos abroad increased 500 percent.) Through the tax amnesty to backsliders, and new simplified tax forms, the IRS pulled in over four billion pesos ($666 million) in 1972, tripling the previous year's collection.

The second biggest tax loophole was in real estate. Collusion among buyers, sellers, and assessors, and the avoidance of capital gains was routine—especially in rural areas where the land was held by wealthy absentee landowners who saw to it, through their political influence, that they were not heavily taxed. The assessors "hardly moved," according to Virata, and assessments were left uncompleted. "Property values were declared very low for tax purposes—but very high when it came to collateral purposes!"

The national government had never done much about this tax inequity—not only because of its political protection, but also because the recipients of the real estate taxes are the local governments which, in the past, had fallen so far short of meeting the costs of services that the cities were forced annually to tap the national government for aid (which it supplied from IRS proceeds). In Manila the city government might collect as high as eighty percent on real estate—while the overall country would collect only forty-five percent. In the year 1972, after the corrupt assessors were weeded out and an improved method of assessment introduced, the collection of real estate taxes increased an astronomical sixty-seven percent in the rural areas, and twenty-nine percent in the cities —taking the pressure off the national government and freeing its revenues for other projects. Now that he has successfully shaken up the tax structure, Secretary Virata is currently trying a "self-policing" system, where owners are obliged to declare the realistic value of their property. (If they declare it obviously too low, the government steps in and offers to buy at that price.)

During the year after martial law was declared, the Bureau of Customs recovered $28 million worth of contraband goods, which included around $1 million in blue-seal cigarettes. At first offering the cigarettes for auction, the department officials soon realized they were only circling them back onto the black market. Now the cigarettes are distributed (free) to inmates of prisons.

The haul also included large quantities of drugs (which were all burned, avoiding such an embarrassment as was faced by the New York City police department when its heroin cache was stolen), PX and commissary items, fake U.S. dollars, heavy vehicles and equipment, and illegal firearms.

It has been said that President Marcos is a political chess player who never makes a move without having thought out the next six. Nowhere was this approach more in evidence than by the decisive actions which the President took immediately after proclaiming martial law. The day following the proclamation, Marcos issued a presidential decree creating a plan for the entire restructuring of the government itself (a reorganization plan prepared by the National Economic Administrative Director, the MIT-trained economist Dr. Gerardo Sicat, which had been offered to the Congress and which Congress had been sitting on). The plan had three basic features: the decentralization of the national government, the standardization of organization, and improvement of the civil service. The fountainhead for the Marcos vision of a New Society lay in the newly created National Economic Development Administration (NEDA) which replaced National Economic Administration. NEDA is headed by Dr. Sicat; it is a tightly structured umbrella authority designed to coordinate all the departments of government involved in the sweeping social reforms Marcos envisioned. It is NEDA that "puts it all together," being charged as it is with drawing up both the long-range as well as the annual plans and programs for the country's social and economic development. Prior to the creation of NEDA, economic and social policies were determined in sometimes unrelated bits and pieces by seven or eight separate agencies. (At the same time an amendment was added to the Central Bank Act enabling the government to respond quickly to monetary crises.)

When the NEDA board meets, the President himself serves as it chairman, with the Secretaries of Finance, Trade, Agriculture, Industry, Education, Labor, and Public Works all present, as well as the Budget Commissioner, the Governor of the Central Bank, and Chairman of the Board of Investments.

Through NEDA all plans for the development of the country are created, coordinating all departments involved. The Board of Investments, under the direction of Secretary of Industry Vicente Paterno, which oversees both foreign and domestic investment, provides a task force to guide would-be investors, a "one stop shop" as Asia's *Business and Industry* calls it, that hand-holds from conception to ground-breaking, freeing the investor from red tape.

Foreigners were the first to react to this new efficiency in the Philippine government. Accustomed to dealing with other authoritarian governments in Asia, such as Taiwan and Singapore, foreign businessmen seized on the chance to deal quickly and efficiently. With no payoffs or delays, they can go directly to the man in charge and get a fast answer. The President himself sees many overseas investors. An American businessman who does business with developing countries throughout Asia said that he was able to accomplish in three days what it had taken him two weeks to do on a previous visit, three years earlier. "Now you can get directly through to the men in charge, and they in turn refer you directly to the top men in other departments. There's no redtape, no cooling your heels in the outer office, and—no payoffs."

Filipino businessmen, on the other hand, who were accustomed to dealing only through politicians, did not know how to handle this streamlined process at first. "They were at a loss for several months," said Secretary Virata. "They didn't know how to stand on their own."

One of the major problems facing the Philippine government in its attempts to restructure its society and put the developing country on the road to economic and social stability was how to make "progress" reach the common man. Economic plans efficiently carried out can always create prosperity at the top, and an increased GNP. But how does all this affect the life of the man at the bottom, the mass base, which is poor? Will Rogers once observed that money, unlike other items that reflect rules of gravity, persists in flowing uphill ("Put a nickel in the store on Monday and it will be in John D. Rockefeller's pocket on Friday").

Robert McNamara, president of the World Bank, made the same point about countries in the recent monetary conference in Nairobi, Kenya: ". . . despite a decade of unprecedented increase in the gross national product of the developing countries, the poorest segments of their populations have received relatively little benefit. . . ."

In the Philippines, where the economy is basically agrarian, "the poorest segment," the mass base representing eighty percent of the total population, is involved in agriculture. Beginning, then, from that fact, the problem confronting the Philippines was how do you go about building up an agrarian base, to raise the standard of living of the majority? Raising minimum wages, for instance, has no effect on the farmers. How can national income be redistributed so that it reaches these people whom it never reached before? And—most important—is it possible to reach down to this level and offer sufficient development at that base to create out of it a middle class?

"Whatever progress had been made in the past in the Philippines never seemed to filter down to the common man," noted presidential Executive Secretary Melchor. "Since this is an agrarian economy, we needed to start from that fact. We have to build up the agrarian base by raising the standard of living there—through land ownership, credit facilities, electrification, and the like—and then set up industries around this base, that relate to its agricultural produce."

The problem of redistribution of income in the Philippines has, therefore, centered on the farmer. Through increased irrigation facilities and instruction in better management which allows for double-cropping, for instance, there is both more work and more income for the individual farmer.

Sustained year-round employment is being developed through local cottage industry. To offset the traditional apathy generated from the sharecropper status (when keeping on good terms with a landowner was more important than high crop yield) and the "disaster syndrome" which causes Filipino farmers to resign themselves to annual crop devastation from natural disasters, the government has also embarked on a vigorous weather modification program, which includes rainmaking operations, typhoon moderation, early storm warning devices, flood control, and reforestation.

In the only before/after study which has thus far been made of a barrio where sharecropper tenant farmers have become landowners, changes in attitudes toward the land was as much in evidence as higher income and standard of living. The study, made by a Japanese researcher from the University of Tokyo's Institute of Oriental Culture, also gives some clues as to why Philippine crop yields have been, in the past, among the lowest in Asia. Comparing the Filipino peasant farmer (before land reform) to the Japanese farmer, the observer noted that, unlike the Japanese, the Filipino tenant farmer showed little emotional attachment to his land, or much concern with its productivity. There was much bad management of the land and avoidable waste, yet the Filipino invariably blamed low crop yields on the weather. The local custom in the barrio was for the tenant and his wife to get other jobs elsewhere whenever they could, and rely on hired help to work the land, which was then charged to the landlord. The usual financial arrangement was that fifty percent went outright to the landlord for the rent of the land and most of the remaining fifty percent also was taken by the landlord to pay present and old debts. Since the landlord was the only form of credit available to him, the tenant and his wife usually had to take jobs outside their home in order to get the cash they needed. When the crop was harvested they shared it with their neighbors and were apt to end up buying rice for their own family, before the next harvest.

After the tenant had become a leaseholder (in the original land program this was the first step toward ownership), the Japanese observer noted, the farmer began to show an active interest in both the productivity of the land and the price of rice (which had not previously affected him, since he did not participate in the sale). In order to manage the land better, and try to get a bigger crop (and thus more sales), he gave up his outside job and, with his family, worked the land himself instead of using outside labor. When the rice was harvested he kept it for his own use and did not give any to his neighbors unless they had actually helped him. With cash from the crop sales at his disposal, he renovated his house, bought farm implements and work animals, a sewing machine for his wife, fighting cocks for Sunday games, and set aside money for his children's college education. In this barrio in Bulacan, six years after the land reform program had been implemented, the overall community also reflected the change. Motorized transport (pedicabs) had replaced *carretelas* (horsedrawn carriages). There was more travel between barrios, and, in general, farm families were wearing better clothes. Rural electrification had appeared in the area, and home radios were now common.

Another thrust of the government's plan for the redistribution of wealth is directed at the people who already have money, in an effort to channel their wealth into productive activities instead of letting it lie unused. Through the increased taxation of land, excessive land ownership is being discouraged. ("Non-productive, untaxed land," explained Dr. Sicat, "is wealth in hiding," which does no good for the economy of the country.) Earlier distribution of wealth is also being encouraged through a donors' tax which is forty percent lower than the inheritance tax.

Foreign investment, which relates to the direction in which the country wants to go, is actively sought and encouraged, especially in such labor intensive activities as the electronics industry, food-processing, and garment industries, which will accelerate employment. "Our poor image will be overcome in this year and the next," predicted Dr. Sicat. "Soon the Philippines will be seen as a land of business opportunity to foreigners."

To equip workers for the jobs which are becoming available as industry is developed has also required a restructuring of the educational system. One of the excesses of democracy as the Philippines has practiced it was the unrealistic professional aspirations of the majority. In a country which spends one third of its national budget on education, the social and economic results of higher education for everyone was severe underemployment of educated people. Doctors ended up taking jobs as male nurses. Lawyers drove taxicabs. Now the government is pressing for a more realistic educational system which stresses vocational rather than academic training. Two hundred and fifty trade and business schools under the Bureau of Vocational Education are now graduating 15,000 skilled workers and technicians annually to work in the fields of agriculture, fisheries, and furniture, electrical, and garment industries. Out of this skilled labor pool the social planners envision the development of a working middle class.

The government's present "four-year development plan," which went into effect in the fall of 1973, one year after the declaration of martial law, is even more ambitious than the initial revamping program. While continuing the original reforms, and improving the agricultural production, this second line of action accelerates the creation of employment and diversification of exports through industries that process the country's raw materials. Sugar, for instance, which is the country's primary export, will now be processed into confectionary items. Instead of just getting the price of logs, which were formerly exported to Taiwan and Japan and processed there, the Philippines will get greater economic use of its wood resources by making plywood, veneers, and furniture for export. The country is already into wood-processed items to such an extent that they actually had to import some logs from neighboring Indonesia (which would not have been necessary if the government had set up appropriate controls in the logging business a decade ago). "But that's all right," said Dr. Sicat. "Because it means we are moving to a new level of the problem."

Industries that convert copra into coconut oil, abaca into paper; copper into ingots, plates, and sheets instead of ore; limestone into cement; and glassware out of beach sands are also being developed.

The price of this trade shift, from supplier of raw materials to exporter of finished and semifinished products, is a rising cost of living, as enormous capital investment is laid out to establish local industries. But the long-term gain will be full employment. "What we want to wipe out is the excess of under-employment," explained Dr. Sicat. "If our strategies are successful—as I believe they will be —in this decade we will reduce significantly the excess labor." There are many countries in Asia that already enjoy full employment economies, Sicat points out: Singapore, Hong Kong, Japan, and Taiwan do. South Korea has almost reached that point. Sicat sees nothing unrealistic about the goal of full employment for the Philippines.

As the country shifts from an agricultural economy dependent on export of raw materials, to a mixed agro-industrial economy, which exports processed goods, its economic dependency picture is also changing. While formerly eighty percent of its exports went to the United

States, in 1973 only thirty-five percent went there, and another thirty-five to forty percent went to Japan. ("We now have two umbilical cords instead of only one," smiled Sicat.) The rest went to other Asian countries and to Europe. The products that now provide the major export income—sugar, wood, coconut, and minerals—will not provide the country's largest expansion in the future, predicts Sicat. While "we will continue to depend on a growing volume of these products [at around five percent annually], we are looking for a changing basket of export commodities" which the government planners hope to see increase at a twenty-five percent rate. Socially this increase is of much more interest to the overall development of the country, since it creates jobs (while increased sales in sugar, coconut, etc., are reflected in the individual grower's wealth).

One piece of luck, in line with this strategy, came when abaca (hemp), once used for rope, which has not been in demand for the past twenty years, reemerged as an important export item when the natural fiber was found to be of value for the production of high-quality paper which is used in paper money and airmail paper. Abaca plantations are being revived (some had already converted to bananas and citrus) and a company has been set up to process the pulp into paper.

At present the major thrust of NEDA's industrial plan is to sell the Philippines's labor market to foreign investment, and the government is looking for diversified foreign investment just as it is looking for diversified exports which will also serve to break the islands' economic dependency on the United States. Americans, as could be expected (considering the parity rights they enjoy with Filipinos, which will expire in 1974), are the largest investors and account for eighty percent of foreign equity investment, the bulk of which is in the manufacturing, chemical and processing industries. Taiwan, the Republic of China runs second to America, with 4.4% and Spain is third, with 4.1%. Japan, oddly enough, considering its economic resources, has only a little over ten million dollars invested in the Philippines (compared to America's $800 million). Japan, which leads all other foreign countries in supplying capital for Philippine development, has chosen instead to offer financial aid to a varied list of Philippine projects, in exchange for contracts for a steady supply of raw materials.

To satisfy the nationalists who in the past opposed all foreign investment on the grounds that it deprived Filipinos of business opportunity, an investment law has been set up which provides for notification to Filipinos of the areas in which expansion and investment is needed. If in three years nationals have not expanded in that area, then the government opens it to foreign investment. An Investment Incentives Act controls the direction in which investment should go to fit the NEDA plans for the country's orderly development.

Some of the current major industrial projects involve Filipino and foreign capital. Nickel, which has not previously been an important export, is being developed by the Marinduque Mining Company (a Filipino company with Filipino, Japanese, and American capital) on a small, government-owned, previously undeveloped island called Nonoc, lying off the northern coast of Mindanao. To create the (strip) mine and refining plant for nickel, which will be in production in 1974 and is expected to produce earnings of over $100 million worth of nickel exports annually, has entailed the creation of an "instant

city" with port facilities, roads, wells, electrification, housing, schools—even a cinema. Formerly a sparsely populated, primitive fishing village, Nonoc is now a teeming
community which provides employment for 6,000 people,
including, in addition to imported exports, the inhabitants
of that island and all the neighboring ones, who commute
to work by *banca* (outrigger canoes). So many of the area
fisherman have taken construction jobs that, as an American superintendent's wife commented ruefully, "You can't
buy fish here any more!" since all the fishermen have
traded in their fishing lines for hard hats. If the Nonoc
operation proves successful, nickel mines and refining
plants will also be located on Mindanao proper, and on the
island of Palawan.

Flying from Manila to Nonoc, one crosses the vast green
jungles of the large undeveloped island of Samar, the
third largest island in the Philippines. When I asked
Jesus Cabarrus, president of the Marinduque Mining
Company, what was there, he pointed out an interior mining operation which his company operates, and a tiny
coast village, then shook his head. "Beyond that, we
don't know. It's jungle. The monkeys hitch rides on our
elevated wired tracks." One of Cabarrus's whimsical
theories as to why the interior of the large, rich-looking,
and beautiful island is apparently uninhabited is that
weathercasters use Samar as a point of reference for de-
scribing the route of typhoons. "Samar is not itself in the
typhoon belt," he smiled, "but all typhoons are described
as '200 miles north of Samar, or 300 miles west of Samar'
and I think people are afraid to settle there." A second,
less ambiguous, reason is that there are no roads as yet
on Samar.

At the rate it is going now, the Philippines could be

fully developed within ten years, according to a study published in 1973 by the director of the Yale University Economic Growth Center. Conducted by the Comprehensive Employment Strategy Mission, and headed by Yale's Dr. Gustav Ranis, the report concluded that the country could achieve full development—provided the problem of employment continues to be given top priority. Unlike many other underdeveloped countries, the Yale observers found, the Philippines is not poor in either resources or people. The recommendations which were made by the Mission are already part of the government's new four-year development plan: namely to create jobs for the unemployed through the development of industrial goods for export, and to pick up the slack for the underemployed in rural areas by establishing small local industries and cottage industries.

Many of Marcos's critics, among the elite and upper class professionals, say they are currently supporting the New Society because economically it has already proved to be good for the country and it is bringing in sizable foreign investment. However, they contend, a lot of this current progress may be attributable to "just luck." A world sugar and copper shortage in 1973, for instance, boosted prices of two principal exports and put the Philippines in a sellers' market. "If the prices dropped for sugar or copper," they say, "we'd be in trouble. Or if we had typhoons like last year. . . ."

The country has not been without its troubles since martial law was declared. There were typhoons in September 1973 which destroyed thirty-four percent of the rice crop. There was an early summer rice shortage. The price of industrial expansion has been a spiraling cost of living, especially in food items.

So far, however, these crises have not disrupted what friends and critics agree is a booming economy—the first that the little country has thus far enjoyed.

III
People

No amount of economic planning, income redistribution, or industrialization will be meaningful, however, unless it keeps pace with the population growth. Fortunately for the future of the Philippines, the Marcos administration is the first one in this Catholic country to come out officially for population control.

If something were not done—and soon—the prospects for the Philippines would be grim indeed. Already forty-three percent of the population is under fifteen years of age, and each worker supports two dependents. And only forty-three percent of the total working population is employed. By projection, if the current population rate should continue unabated, the economy would demand a 380 percent increase in available jobs by the year 2000. "All our resources will not be enough to feed, clothe, and house eighty-nine million people [the population at that time if the present growth rate continues]," warned Dr. Conrado Lorenzo, head of the Commission on Population.

The message of family planning was being carried to the rural population through Secretary Estrella's Department of Agrarian Reform, with the cooperation of Planned Parenthood and World Population Control, even before the government took an official stand on it. Farmers are being educated to the fact that increased food production won't help in the long run if population is unlimited.

Field workers in the land reform movement teach house-wives family planning along with homemaking skills and nutrition.

At first received with silent opposition by the Church, the government birth control program, in which Mrs. Marcos has taken an active leadership, is now receiving its support. In Asia, where, as in Africa and Latin America, nearly half the population is under fifteen, it is estimated (in a report made by the UN Development Program) that not more than one child out of each hundred will have enough food, medical care, and education to become a fully productive citizen (forty will die; forty will suffer brain and/or body damage due to malnutrition). Such a specter of starvation and damaged children has caused Asian Catholics to reject the Pope's stand against birth control as archaic, "an unrealistic approach to a terrible problem." Meeting in Manila in August 1973, bishops, priests, and laymen from eighteen Asian nations agreed that the Pope's encyclical was not infallible, and the majority strongly favored the freedom to practice birth control. The theme of the convention was that the developing nations could not possibly achieve the higher standard of living to which they aspired unless they could curb their galloping birth rates. While frowning on forced sterilization or abortion as means of population control, the Asian Catholics strongly urged all Catholic Asians to "wholeheartedly support all efforts toward the solution of the population problem." They concluded that the Church, at this point in history, "must involve herself with the real problems of the times and commit herself to a search for their solution."

Although it has one of the highest population rates in the world today (a three percent annual growth rate),

Manila street scene

Nipa huts found at the base of the fabled rice terraces of Banaue, engineered by Ifugao tribesmen 2,000 years ago

(on facing page) Muslim worshippers in a mosque in Mindanao

Mrs. Imelda Romualdez Marcos, First Lady of the Philippines

Manila children playing

Discovered in 1971 in a remote jungle in Mindanao, the cave-dwelling Stone Age Tasaday people were found to be living as they had lived thousands of years ago, in harmony with their environment. Asked what they wanted, they replied: "We want nothing because we need nothing."

Malacañang Palace, located on the bank of the Pasig River, is the official residence of the President of the Republic of the Philippines.

President Marcos shaking hands with Luis Taruc, a former Huk commander now working in the Marcos Land Reform Program, and some villagers from Pampanga

the Philippines has a better chance of slowing down its birth rate than, say, India, where population control has been on the books for twenty years, yet never carried out successfully. Although formally espousing it, the government in India continues to "back and fill" and fail to implement aggressively its program because of the pressure from Muslims and Hindus, each of whom suspect that the program is designed to increase the other's majority (just as black militants maintained birth control in the United States was a form of black genocide—a theory later discarded in the face of opposition from black women who wanted the freedom to limit their families).

The present aim of the Philippine government program is to cut the growth rate from three percent to two and a half percent in the next five years. Since the president signed the UN declaration on Family Planning in 1968, over 1000 rural family planning clinics have been established. At first using only medical or paramedical personnel, the program has recently added 2000 "lay motivators," local people trained by the Department of Health.

To give economic teeth to the policy of population control (which was effective in Japan and Singapore) the government has revised the Internal Revenue code so that it provides tax exemption for no more than four children, and the Labor Department has ruled that maternity leaves shall be limited to the first four deliveries only. Instruction in methods of family planning is now included in the curricula of all Philippine medical, nursing, and midwifery schools, and "population education" (as it has been developed through UN/UNICEF) has been introduced into the Philippine educational system. Within the next five years fifty percent of all teachers in the Philippines will have been trained to use "population education" in such elementary school subjects as arithmetic, social studies, home economics, and health, which introduce concepts of population control as it relates to employment, housing, and food supply.

Whether it is the popularity of the Pill to mothers who really didn't want endless deliveries, or the economic incentive that affects both parents, results of the control program are already in evidence. Dr. Clemente Gatmaitan, the Secretary of Health, who has forty-three years' experience in public health work in the Philippines, was surprised, considering the years of Catholic indoctrination, that this first national effort at population control met with so little opposition. "I didn't believe it would be that favorable." By November 1973 over one million people had joined the family planning program (fifty-seven percent of the "new accepters" choose the Pill). Dr. Paulo Campos, the director of one of the Manila medical centers, said, "You can see the effects here already. Our OB wards are half empty this year."

Like other developing countries in Asia and Africa, the Philippines's major health problems (which account for forty-three percent of deaths) are communicable diseases, basically those which relate to poverty and ignorance. TB, for example, which has been eradicated in most affluent developed countries, was until very recently the number one cause of death in the Philippines (it is still one of the highest in the world) and has only this year been nosed out by pneumonia. The relation of national development to the incidence of tuberculosis is shown dramatically in the cases of both Japan and Taiwan, where formerly, as in the Philippines, TB was a number one cause of death, and has now dropped to number seventeen in Japan and thirty-five in Taiwan. Tuberculosis and pneumonia have to do with nutrition, climate, and sanitation. Even today, only fifty percent of the population of the Philippines has a potable water supply, and only forty-seven percent use any form of latrine.

Over half (sixty-nine percent) of the country's children suffer from malnutrition—a reflection of ignorance about nutrition and poor eating habits rather than lack of available food. The Department of Health, Education, and the Department of Social Welfare, under the direction of the Marcos cabinet's one woman member, the articulate and vivacious sociologist Dr. Estefania Aldaba Lim, work together to provide education in nutrition and family planning. Like many of the other Third World countries, the Philippines is using the Mothercraft training program created by Dr. Kendall King especially for developing countries, which educates mothers to grow and feed high-protein local foods (which in the Philippines is mungo beans) and does not require either extensive funding or a food distribution program. Rural schools teach nutrition through their home economic courses, and children learn to grow beans in the school gardens.

Malaria still plagues parts of the Philippines, and, while greatly reduced from eleven million to half a million in the past twenty years, has not yet been eradicated because of the combination of annual floods and a transient population which eludes spray control. Schistosomiasis (snail fever, a disease which became world-known when the United States forces landing in Leyte in 1944 were infected with it) is also endemic to the farm and fishing population of southern Luzon, the Visayas, and Mindanao, who work in snail-infested rice fields and fresh-water streams. A chronic debilitating disease caused by a blood fluke and transmitted through a host snail, this disease takes an incalculable economic toll, since it cuts down on both rice production and man-hours. The Philippines is currently studying the methods in which Japan solved its snail problem through drainage canals, economic development, and population pressure on the land.

A special problem faced by the Philippines's Health Department has been persuading enough doctors to work in rural areas, where housing and living conditions are not attractive. When a twenty-five percent salary bonus failed to lure a sufficient number to carry out the government health programs in the provinces, a ruling was enacted which now requires all medical school graduates to put in two years' service in rural areas. The present health program calls for setting up a network of small twenty-five-bed hospitals, with one doctor plus paramedical personnel, throughout the provinces to handle emergency cases and serve as way stations to large hospital centers. Seventy-one have been constructed this year and 200 more will be completed next year.

IV
The Muslims and Other Minorities

The present government is the first one to create a program designed to integrate the Philippines's non-Christian minorities into the overall national economic and social goals. Rather than attempt to subdue, or simply ignore, them, as has been the policy practiced by the government in the past, the present administration has taken an aggressive and enlightened stand on the country's minority problems. Abjuring a policy of "forced integration," which would attempt to "civilize" and relocate and make little make-believe Christians out of non-Christian tribes, the aim of the New Society is to achieve a cohesive and peaceful—but pluralistic—society which will allow the minority groups to retain their own culture and dignity.

Executive Secretary Melchor, who is serving as head of the government's development task force in Mindanao, which he refers to as "social-economic engineering," taking a one-year-long view, considers the President's handling of the prickly Muslim situation as perhaps Marcos's most outstanding achievement in office.

To begin with, the Muslims were at war with the government. Throughout their history they had been given to periodic flare-ups against whoever was running the country, and this problem was exacerbated at the time martial law was declared by the confiscation of firearms, which unearthed a veritable hornet's nest among the "fight-first–think-later" Muslims. Fearful that the governmental crackdown meant enforced Christianization, many of the relatively uneducated Muslims took to the hills in protest. Encouraged by Maoist agitators and by some foreign Moslem sympathizers, the Muslims' sporadic battling had hardened into a full-scale secessionist movement.

Mindanao, as the secessionists claim, has always been something of "another country" so far as the Philippine government's effort at economic and social development have been concerned. Not only is there a tradition of neglect for cultural reasons, but there has also been the problem of spreading thin what financial resources were available. Government funds have invariably gone first to Luzon and the Visayas, with Mindanao running a poor stepsister third in the allotments. It was also discovered, on closer study, that much of the meager funds which had been earmarked for Muslim Mindanao had ended up in the pockets of the Muslim political leaders whom the government was dealing with. When the government officials in charge of the development of Mindanao discovered the Muslim politicians had lost their credibility, they began dealing, instead, through local scholars and religious leaders.

To convince the suspicious Muslims that the government for once meant them well required a many-sided attack on an ancient problem.

Peace and order had to be established before anything else could be begun. And it was only within the late summer of 1973 that the fighting was sufficiently contained (in Basilan and Sulu) for the government task force to pursue its plans for the resettlement and rehabilitation of the million or more people who were dislocated during the fighting, and launch the development program for the area.

The work was further hampered by the centuries of suspicion and mistrust that have built up between the Muslims and Christians, and their very real cultural differences.

In a number of important concepts Islam and Spanish Catholicism run on a collision course and important concessions must be made by the dominant order to allow the peaceful sharing of a country.

Monogamy is not only the single viable form of martial existence recognized by the Catholic Church, it is also the only form recognized by law in the Philippines, where divorce as well as polygamy, is illegal. Yet the Muslim faith allows the devout to take four wives. Special legal dispensation had to be added to Philippine law which recognizes polygamy and divorce—for Muslims only.

The westernized Catholic is also apt to find his Muslim brother immoral or amoral. Descendants of traders, Muslims' income may be derived from trade with neighboring islands outside the Philippines, such as Indonesia's Borneo. Legally, this barter falls in the realm of smuggling—long a thorn in the side of all administrations. But while President Marcos cracked down on smuggling in Luzon and the Visayas, he has made a special allowance for the continued barter between the Muslims and their neighbors in Borneo simply because it proved in many cases to be their only source of livelihood.

Other important concessions had to be made. When it was discovered how adamant Muslims were about giving up their firearms, and the value—economic and psychological—which they placed on them, the government changed its tactic. Instead of demanding the surrender of privately owned arms, they offered to accept firearms as collateral for land which the Muslim families wanted.

Three additional provinces have been created in Mindanao (which the Muslims always did want done), and an Institute of Islamic Studies has been organized at the Asian Center of the University of the Philippines, which is headed by one of Asia's foremost scholars, Harvard-trained Dr. Ruben Santos-Cuyugan, and is devoted to instruction in and perpetuation of the Islamic language and culture. The judicial wing of the government is also now in the process of codifying the Muslim laws.

While government forces were still engaged in active combat with Muslim insurgents, President Marcos at the same time launched an aggressive offensive on Muslim disorders from a pragmatic, economic level. If Muslim lands can be raised to a par with Christian lands, and Muslim settlers provided a standard of living equal to that of Christian settlers, then much of the age-old antipathy and feelings of injustice can be mitigated.

That the President is on the right track (although lacking funds to see these projects through as fast as he might like) was evidenced when sixty-eight Muslim leaders, including nine captured dissidents, came to Manila in August 1973 to confer with the President about the arrival of a fact-finding committee composed of foreign ministers from five Arab nations.

They met to determine how best the "concerned" Arab nations could help the Filipino Muslims and the consensus was clearly money for the war refugees' care, and to aid in launching the government reconstruction program—most notably the newly instituted bank which the government expects to provide loans at no interest for the Muslim farmers to use to settle and develop agricultural lands.

Especially revealing was the letter presented by the nine former dissidents to the President, thanking him for the humane treatment they received while under detention and pledging cooperation in the future: "We saw that the New Society you wanted all Filipinos to support meant not only courtesy and kindness to us who were under detention, but a new way of life for all our people in Mindanao, Sulu and Palawan. . . . we are with you because you have shown to all our brothers that a Muslim Filipino is not inferior to but an equal of all other Filipinos. . . ."

For once the Muslims were apparently convinced that the government was sincere about promised reforms and promised parity with Christians. It was the first breakthrough in the Muslim impasse which the Philippines has known—and the most hopeful step toward the long-mouthed but little realized integrated society.

"We are seeing for the first time what appears to be the establishment of an enduring foundation towards the solution of what has been a very complex, long-standing problem," explained Secretary Melchor. "The sincerity of the president, his thorough understanding of the Muslim problem, and his comprehensive program for political, economic, social, and spiritual reforms in the region have done much to forge a national consciousness among the Muslims and an awareness that they are a part of the New Society. . . . We are confident that we can transform the basic contradictions of our subcultures into sources of national strength. The principle is simply by making our Christians better Christians and our Muslims better Muslims. . . ."

The secessionist movement has gradually weakened and lost support as more and more Muslims have accepted government aid and more and more trained Muslim professionals have volunteered their services to help the government task force to create a higher standard of living and a better future for the Muslim population.

The remaining seven percent of non-Christian Filipinos range from the Stone Age Tasadays of the Mindanao jungles to the sturdy, industrious (former cannibal) Igorots of Luzon's Mountain Province. The President's talent hunt to locate the man most able and best equipped to take over the unique problems of these non-Christian minorities introduced yet another Harvard man into the Marcos brain trust. This time it was the young, rich, socially conscious Manuel "Manda" Elizalde, who had already devoted years of his own time and much of his own fortune to save the isolated tribesmen of the Philippines from extinction. As secretary of Panamin, the non-profit Foundation to aid Minorities, since 1967, the dedicated, emotionally involved thirty-five-year-old millionaire has performed a herculean job of providing health services, educational facilities, housing, and sanctuary for the non-Christian tribes. At this reading, Elizalde has established eight minority settlements, five schools, and six clinics, as well as set aside 50,000 acres of land reserved for their use. (He has also put in claims on behalf of the non-Christian tribes for another 2 million acres of land.) At the drop of a hint of interest from the palace, the energetic, curly-haired young man flies in planeloads of half-naked tribesmen to perform their native dances for foreign guests—exotic, anachronistic, and often beautiful performances which appear to enchant the performers as much as they do the audiences.

With no formal training in anthropology (his Harvard degree is in business administration), the passionate minority protector will probably find a place in future textbooks for his discovery of the Tasaday tribe whom he has zealously protected from the incursion of both settlers and visitors, providing the modern world with its only glimpse of Stone Age day-to-day existence.

V
Future of the New Society

"When we proclaimed martial law, the Philippines became part of Asia," said Finance Secretary Cesar Virata.

The last of the former colonies in southeast Asia to adopt an authoritarian government, the fact that the

Philippines did adopt martial law is not so surprising to its neighbors as the fact that she was so slow to do it.

A Filipino in International Scouting, who disembarked in Pakistan the day after martial law was declared, was greeted with a laughing throng of Pakistani colleagues.

"What are you laughing about?" he asked them.

"Your martial law," they replied.

"What's funny about that?" he asked.

"What took you so long?" they chuckled.

The Philippine delegate to the Association of Southeast Asian Nations meeting which followed the declaration of martial law was greeted by the representatives of the four other southeast Asian nations with a chorus: "Welcome to the club!"

Its neighbors, Singapore, Indonesia, Taiwan, South Korea have all achieved their peace and order, stability and economic progress through some form of dictatorship or military control. Only twenty years after the Korean armistice South Koreans under the strong-arm of President Chung Hee Park (who rewrote his country's constitution in 1971 in order to stay in office) enjoys unprecedented prosperity through industrialization. Its people are well dressed and fed, the annual GNP has tripled in ten years. A middle class composed of small businessmen and professionals has emerged.

Taiwan, once a tiny outpost of a government in exile, is now a thriving nation which enjoys full employment and an unprecedented economy, which makes any return to the mainland of China irrelevant.

"Filipinos cherished the ideals of democracy," Cesar Virata explained, "and they still do. But unfortunately, a developing nation does not have time for the slow democratic processes. It must have a 'push' to get going."

President Marcos has spoken of lifting martial law sometime this next year. Whether he does or does not will depend to a great extent on the degree to which his New Society reforms appear to be institutionalized. It is the nature of the reformer to want to see his reforms become an irreversible part of the mainstream of society. And Marcos is no exception.

If the government programs are still so young and weak as to be subject to instant overthrow by political forces if the government were changed, then, for the time being at least, there is little doubt that the Philippines will remain "part of Asia."

8

The Threat of Peace:
New Realities in Asia

The Fight for Independence

In 1950, when Philippine ambassador to the United States
Carlos Romulo acting on orders from President Quirino,
sounded out the United States about a proposed conference to be held in Manila to assess the Communist
threat to the emerging countries of southeast Asia, the
United States showed little interest. Romulo was referred
by Secretary of State Dean Acheson to John Foster Dulles,
at that time Acheson's advisor on Asian affairs. Dulles
listened politely to the Philippine proposal, but it was
clear he did not find the Manila conference of sufficient
import for the United States to support it.

Four years later, President Magsaysay called Ambassador Romulo in Washington to report that an anti-Communist alliance of Asian countries and their allies had
been proposed to him by the United States, and he
wanted to obtain the details. By this time Dulles was
Secretary of State, and on this visit Romulo could not

resist reminding Dulles of their abortive meeting concerning basically the same suggestion four years earlier. "As I recall," Romulo twitted the American Secretary of State, "you showed absolutely no interest."

"Now, Mr. Ambassador," Dulles protested, smiling, "don't rub it in."

American foreign policy in Asia immediately following the second World War was dictated by the need to curb the war-making potential of Japan and prevent the recurrence of Japanese hegemony in Asia.

Despite the fact it had granted its former colony independence, America, along with the other western powers, considered the relationship of the great western powers to the Asian nations, following the war, as simply a reinstatement of the former status quo. America's position, siding with the European powers that wished to hang on to their colonies, was made abundantly clear in 1945 when the Charter of the United Nations was drafted in San Francisco.

The original wording of the draft of the Charter referred only to the duty of colonizing powers to promote self-government in their colonies. As the only member of the United Nations from a colony, the Philippine delegation took the position that a serious error was about to be committed. The colonies desired *independence,* not mere *self-government.* The chairman of the Philippine delegation told the United Nations that *independence* was the only word that could give true meaning to the Charter. Without this word, he explained, the Charter would be bereft of meaning to the peoples of Asia and Africa, and kill the hopes of the troubled, despairing, and inarticulate dependent 600 million people who prayed that they would be set free.

The effect of this proposal was to arouse the instant hostility of the western colonizing powers. The United Kingdom, the Netherlands, France, and Belgium led the fight against inclusion of the word *independence* in the draft of the Charter. It was only after bitter debate that a compromise was reached, and the wording of the Charter changed to "self-government *or* independence" as the aim of dependent peoples and which the colonial powers were pledged to promote.

As the first of the great powers to grant a former Asian colony independence, the United States had been, for a time, something of a hero to the small countries of Asia— a position it unfortunately sacrificed when it persisted in supporting the colonial powers against the desire for independence of the small countries. After siding, in the Charter fight, with Britain, France, Belgium, and the Netherlands in their last-gasp effort to maintain supremacy over their Asian colonies, the United States later assumed the same position in its role in the UN trusteeship council. When the United States ambassador to the UN, Francis B. Sayre, the son-in-law of Woodrow Wilson, expressed surprise that the newly independent Philippines voted so consistently against the United States, the head of the Philippine delegation warned him that the "reactionary course" which the United States was pursuing was eroding its prestige in Asia. "The U.S.," the Philippine ambassador told Sayre, in 1947, is "losing prestige and leadership among Oriental people . . . because it is taking sides with the colonial powers at the UN trusteeship council. . . ."

That colonialism was "over" in Asia was a fact known to Asians, but relatively ignored by the west. Despite the recognition of the principle of self-determination in the

United Nations Charter, which was drafted and approved while the war was still in its last stages, it was soon clear that for the western colonial powers the war had not changed anything in Asia.

They were soon to be undeceived. But it was to take more than a decade, at enormous costs of blood and revolution, to make them get the point.

The awakening of the Asian colonies had come, at the outset of the war, when the initial stunning Japanese victories over the western powers had laid to rest once and forever the myth of the invincibility of the west. The destruction of the U.S. Pacific fleet at Pearl Harbor, the sinking of the British battleships *Renown* and *Prince of Wales* at Singapore, the defeat of American ground forces at Bataan and Corregidor, and the easy conquest of British Malaysia and Hong Kong and Dutch Java, had shocked Asia into a new self-awareness which the later defeat of Japan did nothing to dispell. For four centuries brown and yellow Asians had been brainwashed into believing they were inferior to the white western powers, that there was no point in rebelling against the white masters, since they could not be defeated—and certainly never by an Asian nation. When Carlos Romulo, as a graduate student at Columbia University in 1919, warned his American classmates to beware of the threat of Japan, the contemptuous answer was, "Those little two-legged monkeys wouldn't dare attack us!" Those two-legged monkeys, however, under the combined racial and economic offenses of the Exclusion Act and the oil embargo, had spit in the eye of the great America—and won— and it was a victory, no matter how temporary, that Asians would never forget, a putdown of western power which was soon to be reinforced by the breaking of the

American nuclear monopoly by Russia. Later, the launching of the Russian sputnik put the frosting on the cake by showing that the highly vaunted American technology was not supreme, either.

That the Japanese were not unaware of the part they had played in encouraging Asian independence movements was shown in the final days of the war, when Japan chose to surrender its arms to the colonies themselves rather than to the big powers. During the occupation years, Japan had granted these countries a form of so-called self-government, and their manner of exit was in itself a gesture which conferred reality on the fiction of wartime independence.

The end of the war left the Asian colonies thirsting for independence—and seeing it, for the first time, as a clear possibility. The United Nations Charter, with its emphasis on the right of self-determination, added strength to the conviction of the colonies of their legal and moral right to be free.

The first phase of the postwar history of Asia was, then, the struggle for independence. India was set free after bitter fratricidal strife which saw the country split into two. Indonesia fought to recover its own freedom in a long and costly war with the Dutch. Indochina fought the longest war of all, only to emerge divided, and to find itself again at war, both internally and against other powers.

This first phase had hardly been completed—and indeed remains incomplete to this day—when Asia found itself drawn into the vortex of the cold war. The triumph of the People's Republic of China in the civil war of the Chinese people introduced the element which was to alter drastically American foreign policy and dominate

Asian events for the next two decades: the struggle against Communism.

No Asian country failed, in its own fashion, to respond to this new phase in postwar Asian history. India, Indonesia, and Burma turned to nonalignment. The Philippines and Thailand, through membership in the SEATO, became members of the anti-Communist alliance.

The effect of the Communist resurgence and the responses to that threat by the former colonies was to delay the sentiment, still only dimly perceived at this point, for regional unity.

Before western intervention, southeast Asia had been a kind of cultural and political crossroads, where the stream of influences which flowed from the Middle East, India, and China converged. All such ties were severed by the coming of western imperialism, when the centers of allegiance switched to such western capitals as Madrid, Washington, London, Paris, Brussels, and The Hague, even while libertarian movements were incubating in Asia.

Once the former colonies were liberated, however, they found common cause in common problems, especially in the effort to eliminate colonialism throughout the world, and in the solution of their immense economic problems which in many respects derived from the shared experience of colonialism.

The first efforts at forging regional unity were, not surprisingly, colored by the Communist threat. In 1950, in the face of the Huk uprising, President Quirino took the initiative of convening a conference of south and southeast Asian countries primarily aimed at gaining psychological support for the Philippines's internal struggle from neighbors and allies. Quirino had hoped for United States support in this initial conference, but when America declined, he went ahead anyway.

In order to woo neutralist India and Indonesia into the meeting, the Philippines broadened the base of the conference objectives, from a purely anti-Communist grouping into a conference designed to explore the regional problems common to all participants. A subsequent conference was held that same year, in New Delhi, to discuss the freeing of Indonesia from the Dutch.

Five years later, in 1955, Indonesia convened an even more ambitious regional conference at Bandung, which was attended by representatives of twenty-nine Asian and African countries, including the People's Republic of China as well as the neutralist countries. The Bandung Declaration was in many ways a successful compromise, embodying the views of the aligned, the nonaligned, and the Communist states on such unexceptionable issues as self-determination, peaceful coexistence, and economic development.

These three separate attempts at forging regional unity were alike in one respect: they failed to set a pattern for regular meetings. The Bandung Conference *was* intended to become a regular event, but it became instead a vehicle for the expression of purely nonaligned views or the views of the entire Third World. The three Asian conferences, at Baguio, New Delhi, and Bandung, were important, however, as pioneering efforts. They also showed the considerable difficulty of forging a regional political unity in the face of widely divergent views on the issue of Communism. It was clear even then that a successful start at regional unity would require another basis. It was equally clear that the problem of unity could not be attacked frontally without risk of emphasizing the sharp divisions among the countries. The concept of regional unity had to be given time to ripen.

The Bi-Polar World

The triumph of Peking in the Chinese civil war, in 1949, drastically changed United States objectives. Just as the containment of Moscow became the cornerstone of United States policy in Europe, so the containment of Peking became the foundation of United States policy in Asia. The containment doctrine acquired global application, and the cold war spread to all corners of the world.

When the Korean war erupted in 1950, ideological divisions sharpened. In the United States, Japan, instead of being regarded as a potential enemy, began to be viewed as an anti-Communist bastion. Strong support was also given to Taiwan as a symbol of anti-Communist resistance and to provide an alternative focus for Chinese allegiance.

The United States policy was much less clear in regard to the other Asian countries, except in one thing. They were important in American eyes in proportion to their usefulness in pursuing United States policy objectives in Asia. Some were courted, others kept under the American wing, still others designed to be "saved" from the evils of Communism.

The fall of Dienbienphu, ending the French regime in Indochina—and terminating the reign of the last great western colonial power in Asia—forced the United States to initiate the second phase of its campaign to halt what it viewed as Communist expansionism in Asia, a regional umbrella security, the Southeast Asia Treaty Organization, SEATO.

When the United States broached the idea of forming this anti-Communist alliance, in 1954, Ambassador Romulo suggested to President Magsaysay that such an alliance would gain broad support in Asia only if it included a Pacific Charter, similar to the Atlantic Charter. A Pacific Charter which defined the broad principles of the free world alliance would remove the negative character of the proposed alliance and emphasize the long-range objectives to which not only the members of the alliance but other Asian countries could adhere in principle. No one had any illusions that the United States's proposal would meet with general political approval in Asia, but the inclusion of a Pacific Charter was a way of forestalling the expected criticism, particularly from the neutralist quarters.

President Magsaysay asked for time to reflect. Later he called Romulo in Washington back to say that not only did he approve of the inclusion of a Pacific Charter, but that Secretary of State Dulles should be told that the Philippines would join the proposed alliance *only* if the Charter was included.

When Romulo relayed the Phillipine position to him, Dulles said he would ask his advisors to study the question. What subsequently happened is told by Robert Aura Smith of *The New York Times,* in his book, *Philippine Freedom: 1946–1958,* published in 1958 by Columbia University Press:

This was Romulo's special project and chief object of enthusiasm from the beginning. . . . Three years before the meeting in Manila, Romulo had drafted the outline of such a charter on the back of a menu in a New York restaurant. . . . Six months before the Treaty Organization came into shape, Romulo and President Magsaysay went over the text of a proposed declaration of purposes to be delivered whenever such a meeting should take place, and Magsaysay made it public as an objective in Philippine policy. It was on the basis of this text that Romulo made his appeal to the American public. . . .

It was Romulo's position, strongly supported by Magsaysay, that military commitments alone were not enough to meet the Communist threat. It was felt that a clear declaration of good intent was necessary to offset the continuous barrage of Communist propaganda about colonialism. If Western powers and Eastern states could agree to such a declaration a firmer basis for any military alliance could be reached.

There were two assumptions underlying the SEATO. The first was that Communist China was an expansionist power and that the fall of the French regime in Asia and the triumph of the Communist Ho Chi Minh would open the door to Chinese or Chinese-sponsored take-over. It was important, therefore, to draw the line beyond which Communist China could not trespass without provoking United States's retaliatory response.

The second assumption, subsequently called the domino theory, was that if any country in southeast Asia fell to the Communists, the rest would automatically succumb. In accordance with this theory, therefore, any southeast

Asian nation facing the threat of Communism became a major battleground.

Later events especially the debacle in Vietnam, were to make these assumptions questionable and even the inclusion of the Pacific Charter in the Manila Pact did not entirely erase suspicion of United States motives in Asia. Many of the Asian countries felt that the United States was less interested in the overwhelmingly difficult problems of their people than in their usefulness in the struggle against Communism. In any event, they were confident of their ability to deal with their own internal problems of dissidence and were wary of being drawn into a struggle to which they attached less importance than to their courageous but often insufficient efforts to build stable societies.

Whether these views were right or wrong, the fact is that SEATO diminished in importance. By 1972, two of its members, France and Pakistan, had quit the alliance. Other members, notably Australia, New Zealand, and the Philippines, urged that the SEATO begin a face-lifting if it desired to meet the changing requirements of the time.

In the 1972 ministerial meeting of the SEATO in Canberra, Australia, Romulo, who was at this time the Philippine Secretary of Foreign Affairs, said, "In the warmer climate of detente in Asia . . . [the SEATO] is bound to be viewed as an anachronistic and needlessly provocative presence."

He continued, "What the SEATO needs is a massive transformation. It needs to redefine its purposes in the light of the rapidly evolving times. It needs to change its orientation to meet the new requirements of southeast

Asia. It needs to take full account of the popular aspiration to be free from all kinds of interference in internal affairs."

The Road to Detente

As long as the world was divided into two centers of power, the bipolar world of the United States pitted ideologically against the U.S.S.R., the temperature of the cold war remained frigid. It is not easy to fix an exact point in time when the cold war began to abate, but the bipolar concept of power began to be eroded by two widely separated events: the Hungarian rebellion and schismatic break between Peking and Moscow. These marked the collapse of the monolithic structure of international Communism into nationally fragmented forms. Although Moscow retained its tight hold in eastern Europe, its pronouncements were no longer accepted as infallible throughout the Communist world. And indeed Peking destroyed, perhaps forever, the symmetrical order of the bipolar world.

The breakup of the Communist world also caused a resounding reaction in the so-called free world alliance. As its acknowledged leader, the United States found it did not have the same authority over its allies that it had at the height of the cold war. No longer faced with the combined threat of Peking and Moscow, America's allies in western Europe began to think more in terms of their own interests.

Other forces were also at work. The success of the Common Market brought into birth a potential third power in Europe, able to challenge, through its tremendous economic strength, both the United States and the Soviet Union. In Asia, the spectacular rise of Japan as a world economic power reinforced the spreading belief that western power—military or economic—was no longer predominant.

These developments revised the cold war equation. It was no longer possible to think of international affairs in terms of ideology only. The great powers began to behave as great powers with individual interests to protect or to promote, rather than as twin power blocs representing the free world and the Communist world.

It can be said that Moscow's break with Peking, on the one hand, and the relative decline in United States strategic and economic advantages, on the other, led to the détente between Moscow and Washington. Similar reasons led, on the other side of the world, to the détente between Washington and Peking. Each of the three powers involved quite clearly revised their priorities. Peking had to protect its flanks, so to speak, in fear of a possible showdown with Moscow. Moscow, for its part, had to have a secure Europe before it could turn its attention to its problems with China. The United States had to liquidate an unpopular war in Vietnam and at the same time be free to confront the international financial crisis which is bound to test its strength vis-à-vis Japan and western Europe.

The détente among the great powers was born of necessity, a logical result of the internal political and economic dynamics in each of the three countries. But it did result in the common acceptance of two beneficial principles: the renunciation of nuclear war and, in Asia at least, the renunciation of single hegemony in the region.

Nixon Doctrine

On January 2, 1969, Secretary of Foreign Affairs Romulo predicted that the next stage of United States policy in Asia would be a diminution of the American presence in the continent. His statement at the time was viewed, by the United States press at least, as anti-American. Barely six months later, President Nixon proved this forecast correct when he announced at Guam the Nixon Doctrine. Although the Doctrine is ambiguous in many respects, it seems clear that the United States will begin a progressive reduction of its military forces in Asia. Thereafter it will no longer fight any land wars in the continent, but will be prepared to assist in other ways any nation threatened by Communist aggression. It also appears to mean that the United States will retain its strategic nuclear umbrella to balance Communist China's nuclear power.

Insofar as southeast Asia was concerned, the United States appeared to have tacitly reversed Dulles's notorious domino theory. The Communist movements that have characterized most Asian countries operate independently and although they undoubtedly receive encouragement from abroad, they are no longer viewed as parts of a single massive conspiracy. Furthermore, the capability of the countries of southeast Asia to resist Communist insurgence lies in direct proportion to their political and economic stability. This is the real anchor of their security.

Nevertheless, the announcement of the Nixon Doctrine caused some apprehension in southeast Asia. The feeling was that if the United States was removing its military shield from the region, then in all fairness the countries should be given the necessary time to build their own defenses, instead of being left defenseless at a delicate period in the history of the region.

The United States sought to allay such fears. Speaking at the United Nations, Secretary of State Henry Kissinger said, "We will never abandon our allies and friends. The strengthening of our traditional ties is the essential foundation for the development of new relationships with old adversaries."

In Manila the newly appointed U.S. ambassador, William H. Sullivan, a seasoned diplomat who was the right-hand man of Secretary Kissinger in the Vietnam negotiations, issued similar reassurances that the United States did not contemplate withdrawal from Asia but only a reduction of its military forces.

The Asian Response

The emerging picture in Asia today is that of a quadrilateral power balance in which Peking, Washington, Toyko, and Moscow will act as mutual checks and balances, and thus, it is hoped, restore stability to the region. In theory, there is much to be said for this new development, especially if the great powers choose to cooperate not merely in the promotion of their interests but in the promotion of the interests of the developing countries. The equilibrium will diminish chances of Communist aggression, since such an act would disturb the power balance. As far as the developing countries are concerned, a new security will have been established, permitting them to devote their full attention to the urgent tasks of development.

The Threat of Peace

Nevertheless, if the threat of war has diminished, an equally forbidding threat confronts southeast Asian countries today; namely, the threat of peace. After the initial euphoria which followed the Peking-Washington rapprochement, certain misgivings began to assail the developing countries of the region.

The Asians fear, first of all, that the détente is primarily for the interest of the great powers, and consequently the interests of the smaller nations will be sacrificed. Second, they fear that the détente merely signals the renewal of great-power rivalry in other fields and that the chosen battleground is the developing countries. ("Whenever the elephants fight, we are the grass under their feet.") Third, they fear that the détente may result in the division of Asia into spheres of influence among the great powers.

Should any of these situations develop, it could mean a repetition of the cycle of political conflicts, the same conflicts, that caused the tragedy of Vietnam. Alternatively, the region could become an open field for economic exploitation, resulting in a new form of colonialism worse than the classical type.

As great a danger as any of the foregoing in the Asian view is the possibility that in order to avert such direct conflict among the great powers, they would agree among themselves to the creation of spheres of influence. As a cure for conflict, this theory is fallacious according to southeast Asian diplomats, since it would invariably lead to ultimate confrontation. As a means of stabilizing the region, it would prove equally fallacious they argue since it would negate the sovereign status of the small countries and thus raise dangerous tensions of another kind.

The response of the southeast Asian nations to the emerging situation is currently taking the following forms:

First, the countries of that region feel free to make their own accommodations with the Communist world. Second, there is an increased recognition of the urgent need for political and economic unity in the region, in order to strengthen its position vis-à-vis the great powers.

Finally, there is a growing feeling, following the Vietnam war, that there is a need for the region to insulate itself from the great power rivalries while cooperating with them on matters of common interest.

Thus the threat of peace may well usher in a third stage in the postwar history of southeast Asia—a renewed drive toward regional unity. The focus of this aspiration is the six-year-old Association of Southeast Asian Nations (ASEAN). Primarily a grouping for social and economic cooperation, the five-nation confederation, which includes, in addition to the Philippines, Indonesia, Malaysia, Singapore, and Thailand, has begun to concern itself with political and diplomatic unity. It recently issued a Declaration on a Zone of Peace, Freedom, and Neutrality as an expression of its determination to free the region from external intervention in its internal affairs.

In the wake of the Asian détente, Japan has established relations with Peking. So has Australia. For a variety of reasons, the southeast Asian nations have been more cautious in their approach to the problem of normalizing relations with the People's Republic of China. But many of them already have commercial relations with Peking and further rapprochement is probably only a question of time.

As for the Philippines, for the first time in its independent history, it has established formal relations with Socialist countries in Europe and Asia. Well before détente, President Marcos reversed traditional Philippine foreign policy on the question, deciding that ideology should be no bar to relations among nations. Normalization of relations with Yugoslavia, Romania, Poland, East Germany, Czechoslovakia, Hungary, Mongolia, and Bulgaria has followed. The Philippines also has excellent relations in an informal sense with both Moscow and Peking, with both of which it is now contemplating trade ties. Complete normalization of relations is expected to follow.

Like its southeast Asian neighbors, the Philippines is in the midst of an effort to balance its worldwide relations, diversify its markets, and adjust itself to the new realities in Asia.

9
Emerging Identity:
The New Filipino

To assume its proper, sovereign position in the Asia of today and the future requires that the Philippines restructure its national personality as well as its economic and social goals. The profile of the Filipino, modified and often scarred by the various influences of Spanish, American, and Japanese domination, requires a face-lift to meet the challenging demands of the new Asian world.

The apathy, resignation, querulous regional antipathies and personal hostilities of the past have no place in the progressive future course charted by the New Society. To get on the road to nationhood requires revitalization and idealization. It requires, above all else, a national discipline and faith in government, which have been notoriously lacking in Philippine society.

Four centuries of alien rule in which he had no voice or authority rendered the Filipino idealistically and culturally bankrupt. Stripped of his ethnic culture, deprived of political and social autonomy, he tended to have no faith in government, and no civic pride. For reassurance and stability he turned inward to the family unit, putting his trust in kin or patron ahead of country.

The Marcos government is attempting to reach a larger percent of the citizenry than have heretofore participated by lowering the voting age (from eighteen to fifteen) and through a change in the literacy requirements—which formerly excluded nearly forty percent of the adult population. The new constitution, which provides for a parliamentary system of government, is clearly aimed at the creation of not only a New Society but a new national character. For it to work effectively, according to one analyst who made a comparative study of the new and the old constitutions (the old one, written in 1935, was patterned on the United States Constitution), will require "the transformation of the whole personality of the Filipino."

Highly nationalistic and socially oriented, the new constitution provides a progressive ideology which requires national discipline, and the "self discipline essential to national progress," clearly setting up loyalty and duty to the country and society above loyalty to kin and family. It makes the point that putting kinship or provincial loyalties above country resulted in some of the well-known ills of Filipino society in the past: lawlessness, tax evasion, patronage, and warlordism.

Whether or not a strong national spirit and belief in country ahead of kinship or privilege can be developed, and a clear national image welded out of a geographically, linguistically, and culturally fragmented people, is one of the New Society's greatest challenges.

The most alienated and fragmented of all Asians, because of their long exposure to western dominance, Filipinos became the least recognizable of Asians, with the least typically national profile. Easygoing and adaptive, they aped their western rulers, copying their dress and speech and mannerisms until they became known in the Asian community as "brown Americans," considered incapable of original and independent thought. As such, Filipinos became suspect to other Asians, and their leaders suffered lack of credibility in the Asian community. When one of their statesmen spoke before an Indian Council for Cultural Relations, for example, a member of the Indian cabinet confessed to him, "I voted against inviting you here. I couldn't believe a Filipino could deliver a speech of this calibre. I thought you were all dance orchestra men. . . ."

Irresponsible and eclectic, Filipinos borrowed anything that struck their fancy—ideas and tastes as often as clothes and language. And, unlike the Japanese who managed to modernize and industrialize while keeping an ancient culture and tradition intact, the Filipinos lost or let die from disuse what was traditionally their own. Little Filipinos dreamed in technicolored westerns. Matrons passed up their own superb local products for the guaranteed joys of Kraft and Heinz. Local artists languished while wealthy Filipinos dragged home bad copies of European masters.

For the first time, this past year, thanks largely to the efforts of Mrs. Marcos, the Philippines officially recognized and honored its "national artists"—the ranking poets, painters, sculptors—providing them a lifetime pension equal to the pensions allotted former presidents. Also through Mrs. Marcos's efforts, a foundation has been established to provide scholarships for young Filipino musicians. Another of the First Lady's efforts on behalf of the renaissance of a national culture is the development of the Nayong Pilipino, a "native" center near the international airport which displays the crafts, dress, architecture, and food of the various provinces.

To provide the Filipino people with the national pride and push for achievement that a developing nation requires to forge ahead demands an almost total psychological reorientation. Unfortunately, as President Marcos once ruefully pointed out, the Philippines—unlike old, affluent, developed societies such as the United States or the United Kingdom, whose growing pains are lost in history—must go through its agonizing struggle toward nationhood in full view of the entire world, with each slap on the fanny or divestiture of an unappealing childhood habit subject to world view and world criticism.

Products of the colonial syndrome, Filipinos are not accustomed to thinking in terms of responsibility to others, merit, or personal commitment. After martial law was declared and several newspapers were shut down, for example, jobless journalists rushed to get whatever work was available, regardless of former editorial stances. One columnist who had been the protégé of the publisher of a newspaper that was closed and had accepted not only his boss's largesse, but special favors which had enabled him to live in luxury, offered to attack his former patron, explaining that having been on the "inside," he was the best equipped.

When direct government control over the press was lifted recently, the results were "disappointing," according to Secretary Tatad. There was little change in the content, which remained timid and dull. Tatad chided the press, explaining that while the government had closed the press because it was licentious, legitimate criticism was no longer restricted. "Why don't you address yourself to issues?" he asked the newsmen. "Criticism is not confined to denouncing personalities."

To win the cooperation of the people, and inspire the push and drive needed to develop the country, the government must convince the mass of citizens that they are part of it; that the government reflects their interests, and wants their participation in achieving its aims. "And if we can convince them of this, then any temporary restraint of freedoms will be forgiven," explained Executive Secretary Melchor. "For a society to develop, you have to have certain basic minimums of health, education, etc. Then you have to establish an incentive factor, the need to achieve. . . ."

To get the people into high gear, however, requires restructuring the Filipino psyche, just as getting the economy going meant restructuring the economic and social order of the country. It requires discarding ancient apathy, indifference, dependence habits, and creating in their stead a vigorous and independent national spirit.

On the simplest level, this restructure requires ordinary discipline.

Far from the fascist puppet-order discipline the word implies, in the Philippines discipline simply means developing the respect for public places and others' rights, which is taken for granted in most developed societies. Today, slogans in Tagalog dot the highways and thoroughfares of the Philippines with admonitions to "please not litter," "please observe safety"—ordinary rules of public behavior which are entrenched in other countries, but new to Philippine comprehension.

For the visitor, one of the quick lessons in the lack of the ordinary disciplines that make other societies function smoothly is to take a midday taxi or car ride through the downtown Ermita section of Manila where hotels, businesses, and some government buildings are located. Every variety of conveyance fills the narrow streets: horse-drawn calesas, jeepneys, buses, trucks, private cars, motorcycles, and bicycles. No one apparently observes lanes or stop signs. Cars clog intersections, zip through red lights, and cross over traffic lanes. Even under the more austere rules of the New Society, the police stationed at intersections often leave their posts (in despair, perhaps) and let the traffic stand there honking and bawling insults at one another.

That some cars occasionally do stop these days to allow pedestrians to cross pedestrian crossings without having to leap for safety is considered a marvel of progress.

In a country where regional loyalties and mutual antagonisms run deep, the Filipino tends to display a latent hostility to all authority, and views any rule or regulation as an infringement of personal liberty. A Filipino, for example, unlike the disciplined British, detests queues and will go to any length, including begging or bribing someone at the front of the line, to avoid standing in line. Having got ahead by cheating or charming "rulers" in the past and stealing from or killing his occupation oppressors, the Filipino is not conditioned to "pay his share." Newspaper machines that rely on a buyer's honor to leave his change, for example, have not been considered for the Philippines, and the one attempt at parking meters was a total disaster, with hardly a coin to be found in the crop of slugs—and even some of the meters themselves were stolen. A lone attempt to use automatic change containers on a toll road met with a similar fate, as not only slugs but stones of the appropriate weight to trip the device were quickly found by enterprising drivers. A plus on the side of martial law is simply that all Filipinos are forced to obey some specific rules, and learn to accept some specific disciplines. Corruption and special privilege no longer need be accepted as an inevitable way of Philippine life. Not since the days of occupation have Filipinos found themselves all "in the same boat" so far as freedoms are concerned. The curfew, regarded with resentment and skepticism at first, is now favored by large segments of the population. Wives and mothers especially enjoy the family solidarity it has provided. ("We know where our children are.") Club owners and restaurateurs, wary at first about harmful effects on their business, have come around to thinking it a good idea. The owner of one nightclub, which was formerly billed as "After Six," simply added "Before and—" to the club's name, and the orchestra plays without intermission, to the same crowds. After ten months of martial law, the co-owner of a popular seafood restaurant in Manila decided "it's really good for our business. When you can close at a reasonable hour the staff can get home at a decent time and you don't draw the hoodlums who hang around and dirty up the tables just drinking. You get a good family trade that comes for the food."

"A revolution," explained President Marcos, "can afford to make all types of mistakes—but not a moral one." Discipline, as Marcos sees it, must be sharply maintained at the top level so that it will filter down, and inspirit the masses.

In an effort to inspire self-sufficiency, the government officially discourages the old practices of the patronage, godfather social order. Secretary Tatad said that when he gets calls at his office to sponsor baptisms or weddings he explains he would like to but—1) "You're not even sure of my religion," and 2) "We don't even know each other. A godfather or sponsor should not be just a politician who might have some pull when you need it. He should be someone close to your family who can advise you in times of need."

Job recommendations are similarly discouraged. "Go try to get the job on your own merit," is Tatad's advice. "Then, if you do encounter difficulty, let me know what the problem is. Perhaps I can help you. But don't ask for a recommendation."

In the past, the Philippines did not have to be self-sufficient. Its relationship with "mother America" insured its defense, through the presence of the United States military bases, and a market for its principal products through preferential trade terms. When in trouble, there was always America to lean on. There was no necessity of learning how to handle one's self alone against the world. To achieve a healthy independence, the Filipino profile, personally and nationally, has to be sharpened and strengthened. The individual and the country each has to learn to stand on its own feet.

Already Marcos has expressed worries that the first year of the New Society may have been "too good," "too easy." There was no bloodshed. No economic crisis. Nobody got hurt. Complacency, once a "way of life" in the country's political structure, might set in again. "We've got everything the easy way," explained Secretary Tatad. "There's the danger of slipping back into the old ways. Discipline must be maintained—especially in leadership."

A clue that the country may be changing in character occurred early in the summer of 1973 when the government was hit with a rice crisis. The western world may fret over the Filipino's loss of civil liberties, but the country's leaders know that the one way you can really hurt him is to limit his daily rice. In the Philippines governments have literally risen and fallen on the question of rice. More than mere high per capita consumption, rice possesses a mystical power to the Filipino. Traditionally, he rises early, breakfasts on rice and fish (as the president himself does), eats rice at lunch, and again at dinner, regardless of what else may be on the menu. And if the meal is only rice, rice with a bit of molasses, or rice with a bit of fish, he is satisfied. But take away the rice and he feels "weak," "tired," "empty." He can't do his work. During the summer shortage, when the Manila Hilton Hotel gave its staff a lunch of spaghetti and French bread—which fires the energies of French or Italian laborers very well indeed—the Filipinos complained that they "felt hungry" an hour later. They couldn't finish the afternoon's work. A wealthy family, with a staff of twenty-one, offered their servants a meal of expensive imported American beefsteak with potatoes and bread, and the servants moped disconsolately, asking sadly, "Isn't there even a cup of rice?"

But even the clever magician Marcos couldn't pull the rice rabbit out of his presidential hat. In 1971 the Philippines, despite the enormity of its international problems, had enjoyed a surplus rice harvest, with enough rice to feed the country the following year. But the devastating floods and typhoons of 1972, which turned the country's principal ricelands into a disaster area, meant shortages in 1973—a situation which the government duly anticipated, and orders were put in with neighboring Thailand and Indonesia. But the Philippines was not the only country that suffered from natural disasters. Much of the rice-producing land in Thailand was hit, and Thailand was unable to deliver the first prepaid shipment due to the Philippines. Although nobody was starving, the rice shortage was the most critical test of the Marcos administration since the declaration of martial law. The fact that corn was plentiful was little help (despite daily propagandizing and recipes in the newspapers). People were grumbling. A driver who was given a sack of rice by his employer was afraid to take it home in daylight, for fear he would be mobbed by his neighbors.

In the past rice has always been a hot political issue. A neat way to capture a constituency, for instance, was for an aspiring politician, anticipating a shortage, to get hold of a private supply and then dole it out in exchange for a political commitment. Whoever gives the people rice gains their undying allegiance.

With no Congress to deal with, President Marcos felt free to attack the rice problem on a nonpolitical basis. He went to the people and told them the truth. Rice had been ordered but it had not been delivered. There was a shortage. Everyone must wait. They would have to eat corn while they waited. But he would promise them one thing: when the rice arrived it would be fairly distributed. Everyone would get his share. Meanwhile, hoarders would be ferreted out and prosecuted.

It was the first time Filipinos had been asked to accept the truth about a rice crisis, and also asked for the patience and fortitude to wait it out.

It was a situation which old Philippine hands knew could foment a revolution. At the very least an ugly scene, climaxed by a few random deaths.

Nothing happened. The people kept on grumbling

about rice. But they held firm, ate their corn, and waited. Finally, in early August, an alternate shipment arrived from Indonesia. The rice was unloaded and distributed to the cities under armed guard. To insure equitable distribution to families, it was sent to the barangays where the local barangay leaders were held responsible for doling it out to the members of their communities, who had to show their voter registration cards for identification.

President Marcos has been widely criticized by the foreign press for using the barangay as a political unit which, it is claimed, is simply a device to give his "dictatorship" the "appearance of legality." Marcos, however, views its use as a means of involving the citizenry directly with the government. Some surgery was in order, he believes, to sever the traditional tie between the average citizen and the local political boss, who represented the interests of either a congressman or a landowner. He sees the reactivation of the ancient Malay barangay social-political structure as a political modification adaptable to the basic Filipino personality. Like the New England town meeting, the local barangay provides government involvement on a grassroots level.*

Executive Secretary Melchor considers the President's handling of the 1973 rice crisis one of his greatest triumphs to date. "He stopped treating rice as a political

---

* When the barangay was used as a means of citizens' voting directly on government issues in the July 27 referendum, it was charged by *Newsweek* that the barangays were all "manned" by armed constabulary who saw to it that everyone voted the way the government wished. On checking, it was discovered that such a scheme would have been impossible, since the number of barangays exceeds the number of men in the constabulary, even if they had all been assigned to the polling places. In the three polling places chosen at random to visit at that time, one policeman and no soldiers were visible.

commodity. He got the people to 'think rationally and act effectively,' which, as Myrdal has pointed out, is the most important dimension of a country's development.

"The people believed Marcos and they willingly did without rice. This," Melchor said thoughtfully, "I found to be a more resounding support of the people for the president and the martial law reforms he has brought about than the results of any referendum would indicate."

The people's response, Melchor pointed out, shows that Philippine society is actually changing. When the people show they trust their government, the psychological restructuring is already in process. A society has begun to mature when it can accept the truth.

10

The Philippines and the
United States Today

It was formerly said that ninety percent of the foreign policy of the Philippines concerned its relations with the United States. Until very recently, there was a great deal of truth to this charge. To begin with, the relationship between the two countries had existed since before the turn of the century when the Americans assisted in the defeat of the ruling Spanish regime, and then engaged the Filipinos in the war which resulted in the colonization of the Philippines by the United States.

For more than four decades the United States assumed the self-imposed mission of training Filipinos for self-government and eventual independence. But when the Philippines did regain its freedom in 1946, it was under circumstances which made inevitable its continued dependence on the United States. Its economy totally destroyed during the second World War, its peace shattered anew by a brewing Communist rebellion, in fear of future invasions such as that which had victimized it in 1941, and unable to defend itself from external enemies, the

Philippines turned to the United States as the only country able and willing to assist it. Thus the most important treaties the Philippines made with a foreign country were those it made with the United States. They were viewed at the time as essential to Philippine survival. The U.S.-Philippines mutual defense pact, the bases treaty, and the Philippine Trade Act, later to be revised as the Laurel-Langley Agreement, to this day constitute the core of the U.S.-R.P. relations.

In fashioning these treaties, it can hardly be said that the United States acted with complete generosity. They created a twenty-five-year pattern of nearly exclusive dependence on the United States by the Philippines. And they fueled strong resentments among Filipinos who increasingly began to view the treaties as inequitable, unfair, and a threat to the sovereignty of the country.

When the United States draft of the bases treaty was first submitted to the Philippine government, Carlos Romulo, who was then the Philippine ambassador to the United Nations, immediately sent a strong memorandum to President Roxas objecting to the provision that required the leasing of the bases for a period of ninety-nine years. "This is unheard of," he wrote. "In no country has this ever happened. It amounts to a permanent lease."

Vice-President Elpidio Quirino, who was then Secretary of Foreign Affairs, agreed with Romulo. But he said there was nothing he could do to change President Roxas's mind, and he advised Romulo to come home to Manila and argue his case.

President Roxas was at that time under intense pressure from several sides. As the first elected president of the newly independent Philippines, he felt the weight of responsibility for picking up the pieces of the shattered

Philippine economy, and he was counting on the United States for assistance. The Communist-led Hukbalahaps were daily gathering strength in central Luzon, they were ready to defy the Roxas government, and it was evident they would soon gain the capability to take over the country if the economic chaos persisted. When his ambassador to the UN began to present the case against the ninety-nine-year lease clause in the proposed bases treaty, the President interrupted him. "Now, now, Carlos," he protested, "don't rock the boat."

The Philippine Trade Act was supposed to be the key to the economic revival of the Philippines, and on this President Roxas pinned his hopes. Yet the briefest glance at the provisions of the Trade Act would have shown that they favored American interests, or rather, they assumed that the recovery of the Philippine economy was dependent on the enhancement of the opportunities for American investment in the Philippines. However true this may have seemed at the time, the effect of the Philippine Trade Act was to encourage Philippine dependence on the American market, and to prevent the diversification of Philippine production for export. The Act tended, in other words, to perpetuate the existing colonial dual economy and thus block the modernization process.

What was regarded as the most onerous provision, however, was the notorious parity clause which permitted American citizens equal rights with Filipinos in the exploitation of Philippine natural resources. Many Filipinos bitterly opposed the parity clause as a derogation of Philippine sovereignty.

As for the Mutual Defense Pact, grievances arose from the Filipino view that the United States was less than wholehearted in its compliance with the military assistance clauses of the treaty. It was claimed that as a result, the infant Philippine army has not been able to modernize at a pace suitable to expected defense requirements.

The substance of the U.S.-R.P. relationships in recent years has been the continuing effort to remove or amend the onerous provisions of these basic treaties with the United States. The ninety-nine-year clause in the bases treaty was eventually reduced to twenty-five years; and the parity clause was amended by the Laurel-Langley Agreement which permitted Filipinos reciprocal rights to engage in business in the United States.

But the problems remain. An across-the-board reexamination of all existing treaties between the United States and the Philippines is now in progress, in accordance with an agreement reached between President Marcos and President Lyndon Johnson in 1966.

Even before the proclamation of martial law and the subsequent launching of the New Society, President Marcos had already begun making strong efforts to redirect Philippine foreign policy. He wanted a policy which is "development-oriented," a policy which would mesh more closely the most pressing requirements of the Philippines and its relations with the outside world.

"The thrust of our foreign policy," he announced, "is towards economic development as the basis of national progress and stability."

In accordance with this foreign policy line, the Secretary of Foreign Affairs initiated what he termed "development diplomacy." This meant primarily a drive toward the discovery of new markets in an expanding series of new relationships with the Common Market and with the Socialist and Communist countries of Europe and Asia. It also meant strengthened efforts to build the economic cooperation schemes of the ASEAN countries into the beginnings, nebulous as they may be at present, of an integral Asian community designed to improve its bargaining position in trade with the rest of the world.

The reorientation of Philippine foreign policy may thus be seen as the product of a complex of several factors, including the changed political configuration of Asia as a result of the Peking-Washington détente, the increasing requirements of domestic economic and social development, and an escalating demand among Filipinos for a more nationalistic foreign policy based solely on the national interest.

Last year, in an effort to hasten new agreements between his country and the United States, President Marcos urged the United States to elevate the negotiations to policy level. Developments which can be anticipated to change the face of the previous agreements are the Nixon Doctrine of withdrawal of ground troops from Asia, which will affect the United States policy in regard to the American military bases now in the Philippines, and the expiration in 1974 of the Laurel-Langley Agreement which would, unless a new economic relationship is negotiated, leave commerce and trade between the two countries without any formal basis.

Filipinos like to describe their grievances against the United States in the language of polite discourse, as "irritants." In fact, these irritants form the context of the anti-American posture of many Filipino nationalists, in particular the youth. Today's youth grew up without memories of the generous outpouring of sentiment between Americans and Filipinos which occurred during the second World War when so many of them fought together in the hills and mountains of the Philippines against the Japanese invaders. They grew up at the height of the bitter national debate concerning parity, the bases question, the termination of veterans' benefits; and they grew up at a time when it was obvious that the former enemies of the United States were receiving all possible assistance while former allies were ignored.

Paradoxically enough, the revived nationalist movement after the second World War was led by such men as Claro Recto, president of the Constitutional Convention, and Jose Laurel, president of the Japanese-sponsored Philippine Republic during the occupation. Left behind by President Quezon to work with the Japanese occupation authorities if necessary, and protect as best they could the interests of the Filipino people, they were imprisoned as collaborators by American authorities after the War, and tried by military tribunal. Although eventually acquitted by the People's Court and saved from prison, the experience angered them and they sought vindication from the people in political office. Laurel, after having nearly won the presidency from incumbent President Quirino, was subsequently elected senator of the Republic. Recto also won a Senate seat, from which privileged position he waged a relentless battle against the unequal provisions in the treaties between the Philippines and the United States. Laurel led the delegation which negotiated the revision of the Philippine Trade Act, which bears his name.

Although neither man won the highest executive position of the Philippines, Laurel and Recto left a lasting legacy, for their insistence on Philippine sovereignty helped mold the minds of the generation which succeeded them. It is unfortunate that they were classified as anti-Americans, for they waged their battles not against

Americans as such but against any derogation of the principle of national sovereignty. Their arguments were never successfully refuted, and the same arguments were used with the same telling effect by their successors.

In recent years a less hysterical form of nationalism has begun to color Philippine foreign policy. This is less a matter of rhetoric than of the recognition that the time of maturity is at hand. The Philippines realizes that it must solve its own problems in the light of its own national interests, and that its interests are not necessarily served by the existing "special relationship" with the United States. The question of national interest has undergone closer scrutiny, for the exigencies of the cold war had blurred the outlines of the specific national interest in favor of the broader interests of the so-called free world.

While clearly a friend of the United States, President Marcos has a nationalist background which promises that the nationalist orientation of Philippine foreign policy will henceforth be pursued with vigor. Perhaps out of consideration for American sensibilities, Filipinos are content to speak of a distinctly Filipino foreign policy rather than a nationalist one. But the content is the same.

Yet a "Filipino" foreign policy does not mean the renunciation of ties with the United States. On the contrary, the assumption is that relations with the United States will be stronger if they are based on mutual respect— a respect lacking as long as the present treaty inequalities exist, and as long as the Philippines is tied to the United States on terms of excessive dependence.

Speaking of the treaty review now being undertaken by the United States and the Philippines, President Marcos's foreign secretary said:

"We feel that these long-pending negotiations could be brought a stage further and firm agreements reached on certain aspects which will provide a new basis for strengthened relations between our two countries. The resumption of negotiations cannot come at a more appropriate time, for though the situation in Asia is in flux, the basic drive towards stability and order is discernible.

"In such a situation, the United States and the Philippines can view their respective interests with an objective eye, resulting in agreements more fruitful to the spirit of friendship than has been possible before. In any case, we feel that the Nixon Doctrine has made it inevitable that the renegotiation of our treaties with the United States should be undertaken at this time."

The fundamental points of the present foreign policy of the New Society are, first of all, the strengthening of relations between the Philippines and the United States on the basis of equality and mutual respect. Then the Philippines seeks to reach out to the rest of the world by normalizing relations with the Socialist and Communist countries; improving its ties with Japan and Australia; pursuing regional unity with its neighbors in southeast Asia; establishing new ties with the Common Market countries; and strengthening its relations with the countries of the Middle East. "The emphasis of the New Society, as declared by President Marcos, is on development," explained the Philippine foreign secretary. "Consequently, the main thrust of our foreign policy is how to adjust our relations with the outside world in ways which will serve the developmental needs of the Philippines. Our main tool is development diplomacy—a policy which encompasses the economic, social, and cultural aspects of our relations with the world."

The decision to open relations with the Socialist world was in part motivated by economic considerations, and by the present need to expand trade and diversify export products. This need has become urgent for the Philippines in the face of the 1974 termination of the Laurel-Langley agreement with the United States, which leaves the character of the trade relationships between the two countries still undefined.

In an oblique reference to the economic relationship between the Philippines and the United States, the Philippine foreign secretary rationalized the economic aspect of ties with the Socialist countries in these words: "We cannot," he said, "knowingly tie our hands and deliberately restrict our freedom in our search for ways of realizing the goals of our society. . . . We hope to universalize our relations, regardless of creed, religion or ideology."

In respect to the Common Market countries, the Philippines has begun a dialogue which it hopes will ultimately lead to the lowering of tariff barriers in favor of basic raw materials such as coconut and coconut products.

The members of ASEAN have already begun to organize for the purpose of protecting the important raw materials of the region, such as rubber in the case of Malaysia, tin in Singapore, lumber in the Philippines. Having decided to speak with a common voice on matters of common interest, the organization is taking concrete steps to protect their primary products in the world market, and at the same time avoid wasteful competition among themselves. At this time in history, when there is as yet no internationally agreed upon law of the seas, the Philippines has also put forward (to the UN) the concept of an archipelagic state (a doctrine supported by such other island nations as Indonesia, Fiji, and Mauritius, with the backing of China, and opposed by such land and maritime powers as the U.S. and U.S.S.R.) that would define all waters around, between, and connecting the outermost islands of the archipelago as part of the sovereign state. Thus all waters contained within straight base lines, drawn from the outermost islands, would no longer be considered international waters (with rights of passage and rights to the wealth beneath the sea shared with other nations) but as part of the political, economic, and geographical entity of the state.

All these recent developments suggest an independent posture in the foreign policy of the Philippines which Americans are called upon to view with the same realism that they view the changes in their own policies. In however negative a fashion, America's less than fair treatment of their former wards in the Pacific (a description which brings the taste of bile to the mouths of contemporary Filipinos) has helped to develop maturity and balance among Filipinos, and has caused them to cast the cold eye of realism on their relations with the outside world. The notorious colonial mentality that kept the Philippines, not necessarily through its own fault, tied to the apron strings of Uncle Sam, is passing away, to be replaced by a new poise based upon self-confidence.

The Philippine foreign secretary summed up the new trend: "Since it takes account of our peculiar needs and expresses our new ideals—in a word, the complex sum of the factors which we call our national interest—the foreign policy of the New Society is more distinctly Filipino than it has been since we regained our independence. To say that the foreign policy of the New Society is independent is merely another way of saying that it has finally become mature."

As a maturing country, the Philippines is also less concerned than formerly with the criticism of the outside world. Long ago resigned to bad foreign press, especially from the United States, the Philippines is too busy forging ahead these days, and solving its own problems, to care much any more. Recently when, after recurrent attacks on the Marcos regime by *The New York Times,* the *Times* man in Manila met with the Philippine foreign secretary for lunch, and brought out his notebook, the secretary waved it away. "Why don't we just enjoy our lunch?" he smiled. "We know you will write something unfavorable about us. We take that for granted now. Write anything you want. But let me tell you one thing—no matter what you write, you will find us still here, just as we were in 1521!"

This new note of independence was also voiced by veteran columnist Teodoro Valencia, of the Manila *Bulletin:* "If we had done all that America wished—and failed—all their approval would not keep us going. And if our present government does prove successful [despite America's qualms and criticisms] then America will be the first to congratulate us! The Philippines," Valencia added wryly, "is not trying to win a gold medal from America. . . ."

The United States foreign policy itself is changing in regard to the developing countries. As Secretary of State Kissinger explained it, America "is no longer on a crusade."

The United States has ceased to tilt with Communism as though it were the world's only evil. Nor does it, today, assume that carbon copies of the American system of government are necessarily the one answer to the problems of developing countries. When he left Vietnam, Ambassador Ellsworth Bunker, who has viewed at first hand the problems inherent to the governments of Argentina, India, and Vietnam, commented: "I have always said that countries like Vietnam, and the countries in South America, should not be expected to model themselves on us and our democratic form of government. . . . They should choose their own kind of government."

That the United States State Department is not unaware of the new impulse for independence and self-determination on the part of the Philippines was indicated when the new United States ambassador to the Philippines, William H. Sullivan, appeared before the Senate foreign relations committee, at the time of his confirmation:

". . . It would be arrogant," Sullivan stated, "for representatives of countries with one form of democratic experience to dictate the exact form the democratic process should take in other countries. . . ."

Whether President Marcos chose correctly for his country, in electing to use martial law as the catalyst for its long delayed maturity, only time will tell. That something in the nature of a Socialist revolution had to take place seems uncontested both by the prior chaos and the subsequent gains. What remains up for question is whether martial law is ever justified as the means of averting anarchy and the possibility of a bloody revolution, and, once instituted, can it in truth ever be only a temporary expediency. Who and what will decide when the need for it is over?

Whatever the answer to that, however, there is little doubt, in either the Philippines or the United States today, that America's former ward is finally "on its way" to becoming a country with which the whole world must reckon.

Index